ISBN: 0-9772923-3-9
ISBN 13: 978-0-9772923-3-2

You can visit us online at: ***www.GrowingWithGrammar.com***

Copyright 2006 by JacKris Publishing, LLC. All rights reserved. No part of this publication may be reproduced or transmitted in any form or by any means, electronic or mechanical, including photocopying, recording, or any information storage and/or retrieval system or device, without permission in writing from the publisher or as authorized by United States Copyright Law.

Printed in the United States of America.

Ver. 2.0.0

Copyright 2006 Growing With Grammar Level 4. All Rights Reserved

How To Use This Student Workbook

Each lesson in this Student Workbook has a corresponding instructional lesson in the Student Manual. Each lesson in this workbook should be completed after the student has read the applicable Student Manual lesson. To reinforce previous concepts learned, most workbook lessons include a few review questions relating to previous lessons. You will also notice that there are small chapter numbers in parentheses after each question. Use these chapter numbers to refer to previous chapters in the Student Manual to which the question pertains.

Copyright 2006 Growing With Grammar Level 4. All Rights Reserved

Copyright 2006 Growing With Grammar Level 4. All Rights Reserved

Worksheet 1.1 (Subjects and Predicates) Name______________________

A. Decide whether the **complete subject** area or the **complete predicate** area is underlined in each sentence. Write **complete subject** or **complete predicate** on the line. **(1.1)**

1. Dad made ice cream. ______________________
2. The burglar hid from the police. ______________________
3. The large squid squirted ink. ______________________
4. The dinner bell rang. ______________________
5. Uncle Joe catches fish. ______________________
6. He finished the game first. ______________________
7. My cousin goes to camp each summer. ______________________
8. Todd dropped the ball. ______________________
9. We helped the injured man. ______________________
10. The dog chased the goose. ______________________

B. Underline the **complete subject** in each sentence. **(1.1)**

1. Mary balanced on one foot.
2. Many cowboys worked on the ranch.
3. Grandpa George fixed the fence.
4. The young girl told funny stories.
5. The book fell off the table.
6. Birds build nests.
7. Joel climbed aboard.
8. One boy rides on the train.

Copyright 2006 Growing With Grammar Level 4. All Rights Reserved

C. Underline the **complete predicate** in each sentence. **(1.1)**

1. Cheryl wrote quickly.
2. The large black bird flew.
3. Cameron read the beautiful poem.
4. The red sun sinks slowly in the sky.
5. The small child cried.
6. I eat the right food.
7. The spacecraft roars.
8. Ruth ate lima bean soup.

D. Identify whether each group of words is a complete **sentence** or a **fragment**. Write **F** for fragment. Write **S** for sentence. **(1.1)**

1. _____ Joy made soup for lunch.
2. _____ Charles likes the carnival.
3. _____ The high cliffs.
4. _____ The sick girl sneezed.
5. _____ Is painted red.
6. _____ Build nests.
7. _____ Louisa dropped a plate.
8. _____ Did not break.
9. _____ Brown bears.
10. _____ Went to the store.

E. Make these **fragments** into complete sentences by adding your own complete subject or complete predicate. **(1.1)**

1. ____ is valuable.
2. The sick child ____.
3. ____ grew in the garden.
4. ____ is from my pen pal.
5. The owl ____.

Copyright 2006 Growing With Grammar Level 4. All Rights Reserved

Worksheet 1.2 (Simple Subjects) Name________________________

A. In the following sentences, each **complete subject** is in bold. Circle each **simple subject**. **(1.1 & 1.2)**

1. **Many oysters** make beautiful pearls.
2. **Two men** searched for buried treasure.
3. **The loud children** woke the baby.
4. **The excited audience** applauded loudly.
5. **My sister Ellen** accepted the award.
6. **Many people** ran in the marathon.
7. **The small black bird** built a nest.
8. **The band** played my favorite song.
9. **My best friend** talks fast.
10. **The chef** baked three cakes.

B. Draw a line dividing the **subject** area from the **predicate** area of each sentence. Write the **simple subject** on the line. **(1.1 & 1.2)**

1. Many beautiful balloons drifted across the sky. ________________________
2. Kara speaks German. ________________________
3. The runner stretched his legs. ________________________
4. That girl told a wonderful story. ________________________
5. Doctor Webster checked my tonsils. ________________________
6. They watched a movie. ________________________
7. Wild horses ran across the field. ________________________
8. Meredith arrived early. ________________________

Copyright 2006 Growing With Grammar Level 4. All Rights Reserved

C. Write sentences of your own using the **simple subjects** in parentheses. **(1.2)**

Example: *(dolphin)* The **dolphin** swims gracefully.

1. *(sister)* ____________________
2. *(snake)* ____________________
3. *(boys)* ____________________
4. *(prince)* ____________________
5. *(bees)* ____________________

D. Complete these sentences by writing a **complete subject**. **(1.1)**

1. ____________________ran down the street.
2. ____________________soared high in the sky.
3. ____________________cried and whined.
4. ____________________is on the table.
5. ____________________asked a question.

E. Identify whether each group of words is a complete **sentence** or a **fragment**. Write **F** for fragment. Write **S** for sentence. **(1.1)**

1. _____ To the movies this afternoon.
2. _____ The tall and shady elm tree.
3. _____ I saw myself in the mirror.
4. _____ Near the train station.
5. _____ Chloe passed the spelling test.
6. _____ Through the window.
7. _____ That long dull movie.
8. _____ She washed the bowl.

Copyright 2006 Growing With Grammar Level 4. All Rights Reserved

Worksheet 1.3 (Simple Predicates) Name________________________

A. In the following sentences, each **complete predicate** is in bold. Circle each **simple predicate**. **(1.1 & 1.3)**

1. Many oysters **make beautiful pearls**.
2. Two men **searched for buried treasure**.
3. The loud children **woke the baby**.
4. The excited audience **applauded loudly**.
5. My sister Ellen **accepted the award**.
6. Many people **ran in the marathon**.
7. The small black bird **built a nest**.
8. The band **played my favorite song**.
9. My best friend **talks fast**.
10. The chef **baked three cakes**.

B. Draw a line dividing the **subject** area from the **predicate** area of each sentence. Write the **simple predicate** on the line. **(1.1 & 1.3)**

1. Many beautiful balloons drifted across the sky. ________________________
2. Kara speaks German. ________________________
3. The runner stretched his legs. ________________________
4. That girl told a wonderful story. ________________________
5. Doctor Webster checked my tonsils. ________________________
6. They watched a movie. ________________________
7. Wild horses ran across the field. ________________________
8. Meredith arrived early. ________________________

Copyright 2006 Growing With Grammar Level 4. All Rights Reserved

C. Write sentences of your own using the **simple predicates** in parentheses. **(1.3)**

Example: *(wrote)* I **wrote** a poem.

1. *(galloped)* ____________________
2. *(discovered)* ____________________
3. *(see)* ____________________
4. *(painted)* ____________________
5. *(forgot)* ____________________

D. In each sentence, draw a line to separate the **complete subject** from the **complete predicate**. Underline the **simple subject** once and the **simple predicate** twice. **(1.1, 1.2, & 1.3)**

1. My family rode the bus today.
2. Cheryl ate a cheeseburger for lunch.
3. The little girl walked to the store.
4. The black car raced down the road.
5. Your bicycle needs new tires.
6. Those girls sing in harmony.
7. The leaves fell.
8. The police helped them.

E. Complete these sentences by writing a **complete predicate**. **(1.1)**

1. The bright sun ____________________.
2. The black bird ____________________.
3. Some squirrels ____________________.
4. Firefighters ____________________.
5. The zookeeper____________________.

F. Write two complete sentences about a visit to the zoo. Draw a line dividing the **subject** area from the **predicate** area of your sentences. **(1.1, 1.2, & 1.3)**

____

____

____

____

____

Copyright 2006 Growing With Grammar Level 4. All Rights Reserved

Worksheet 1.4 (Diagramming Simple Subjects and Predicates) Name________________________

A. Diagram the **simple subject** and **simple predicate** in these sentences. **(1.4)**

1. Hunter read a book.
2. David smiled at me.
3. June helped Kevin.
4. The coyotes howled at night.
5. The apple is red.
6. My mother made lunch.
7. Bruce ate a hamburger.
8. Kim fixed the flat tire.

Copyright 2006 Growing With Grammar Level 4. All Rights Reserved

B. Draw a line dividing the **subject** and **predicate** parts of these sentences. Write the **simple subject** and **simple predicate** for each sentence on the lines. **(1.2 & 1.3)**

1. The beautiful eagle soared. ***subject***_______________ ***predicate***________________
2. Audrey asked a question. ***subject***_______________ ***predicate***________________
3. Skylar planted a tree. ***subject***_______________ ***predicate***________________
4. The nervous girl saw a snake. ***subject***_______________ ***predicate***________________
5. Haley baked a cake. ***subject***_______________ ***predicate***________________
6. My friend wrote a note. ***subject***_______________ ***predicate***________________
7. The colorful fish swam away. ***subject***_______________ ***predicate***________________
8. Many animals live in the forest. ***subject***_______________ ***predicate***________________

C. Cross out the **complete predicate** in these sentences. Then add your own predicate and rewrite each new sentence. **(1.1)**

1. Two men looked for clues.

   ____

2. The pool is so cold!

   ____

3. Three cows grazed in the field.

   ____

4. The artist cleaned his brushes.

   ____

5. Our angry dog chased its tail.

   ____

Copyright 2006 Growing With Grammar Level 4. All Rights Reserved

Worksheet 1.5 (Compound Subjects and Predicates) Name________________________

A. Circle the two subjects in each **compound subject**. (1.5)

1. The children and parents arranged picnic tables.
2. Sandwiches and salad were served for lunch.
3. Corn and beans grew in the field.
4. Mountains and lakes surround the park.
5. The bears and seals made us laugh.
6. Trees and flowers sway in the breeze.
7. Oregon and Maine have huge forests.
8. Lava and ash erupted from the volcano.

B. Circle the two verbs in each **compound predicate**. (1.5)

1. Julie posed and smiled for the camera.
2. Beavers cut and chew trees.
3. Some people ride and race horses.
4. Gina pushes the swing and holds the jump rope.
5. Jacob watches and studies a centipede.
6. Whales live and swim in the ocean.
7. My uncle writes and arranges music.
8. Tamara mops the floor and cleans the bathroom.

Copyright 2006 Growing With Grammar Level 4. All Rights Reserved

C. Identify whether each sentence has a **compound subject** or a **compound predicate**. Write **CS** for compound subject and **CP** for compound predicate. **(1.5)**

1. Louisa dusts the furniture and mops the floor. ____________________
2. Peanuts and peaches grow well in Georgia. ____________________
3. Dogs and ponies marched in the parade. ____________________
4. It was snowing and raining yesterday. ____________________
5. Joshua picked the potatoes and cleaned them. ____________________

D. Diagram the **simple subject** and **simple predicate** in these sentences. **(1.4)**

1. Sam washes the dishes.
2. He drew a picture.
3. Scott fed the birds.
4. The elephant lifted its trunk.
5. Grandma visited yesterday.
6. Teddy painted the ceiling.

Copyright 2006 Growing With Grammar Level 4. All Rights Reserved

Worksheet 1.6 (Diagramming Compound Subjects) Name________________________

A. Diagram these sentences. **(1.6)**

1. Hornets and wasps fly.

2. Jared and Sasha danced.

3. Boys or girls swim.

4. The roses and daisies grow.

5. The lions and tigers eat.

6. Rain or snow fell.

7. The toads and frogs hop.

8. Hannah and Rachel sang.

Copyright 2006 Growing With Grammar Level 4. All Rights Reserved

B. Circle the two subjects in each **compound subject**. (1.5)

1. The bride and groom waved at us.
2. Kimberly and Amanda used the computer.
3. The bus and car stopped.
4. A magazine and a letter arrived in the mail.

C. Change these **fragments** into complete sentences by adding either a **complete subject** or a **complete predicate**. (1.1)

1. Played a game.

____

2. The silly girl.

____

3. Yelled loudly.

____

4. Watered the plants.

____

5. The hungry lion.

____

6. Runs fast.

____

7. Three friends.

____

8. Is in the refrigerator.

____

Copyright 2006 Growing With Grammar Level 4. All Rights Reserved

Worksheet 1.7 (Diagramming Compound Predicates) Name________________________

A. **Diagram** these sentences. **(1.7)**

1. Balls roll or bounce.

2. People sing or dance.

3. Elijah ran and won.

4. The puppy tugged and pulled.

5. The bees buzz and sting.

6. The child smiled and giggled.

7. Diana tripped and fell.

8. The baby slept or ate.

Copyright 2006 Growing With Grammar Level 4. All Rights Reserved

B. Circle the two verbs in each **compound predicate**. (1.5)

1. Cody cooked and ate lasagna.
2. The dog barked and ran in the house.
3. Some people watch and listen to birds.
4. Dad scrubbed and cleaned the sink.

C. Underline the **complete subject** in each sentence. (1.1)

1. My cousin Suzanne asks questions.
2. Andrew moved to Idaho.
3. The brave diver swam with sharks.
4. The boy baked cookies.

D. Draw a line dividing the **subject** and **predicate** parts of these sentences. Write the **simple subject** and **simple predicate** for each sentence on the lines. (1.2 & 1.3)

1. Joy made a necklace. ***subject***_______________ ***predicate***_______________
2. She spent her money. ***subject***_______________ ***predicate***_______________
3. The white cat purred. ***subject***_______________ ***predicate***_______________
4. The plant drops its leaves. ***subject***_______________ ***predicate***_______________
5. Mike sold his bike. ***subject***_______________ ***predicate***_______________
6. My favorite shirt is blue. ***subject***_______________ ***predicate***_______________
7. The talented chef made soup. ***subject***_______________ ***predicate***_______________
8. Kristin ate chicken for dinner. ***subject***_______________ ***predicate***_______________
9. The dog is friendly. ***subject***_______________ ***predicate***_______________
10. Myra built an airplane. ***subject***_______________ ***predicate***_______________

Copyright 2006 Growing With Grammar Level 4. All Rights Reserved

Worksheet 1.8 (Combining Sentences) Name________________________

A. **Combine** these sentences to form a **compound subject**. (Use the conjunction **or** in at least one sentence.) **(1.8)**

1. Ken wanted a salad. Daniel wanted a salad.

____

2. Sam read a book about pigs. Jennifer read a book about pigs.

____

3. You should stay here. Jed should stay here.

____

4. Squirrels eat nuts. Chipmunks eat nuts.

____

5. Doctors work in hospitals. Nurses work in hospitals.

____

B. **Combine** these sentences to form a **compound predicate**. (Use the conjunction **or** in at least one sentence.) **(1.8)**

1. My family went to the movies. My family ate popcorn.

____

2. Dogs will chase balls. Dogs will come when called.

____

3. Jerry hummed the song. Jerry sang the song.

____

4. The puppy jumped. The puppy chased its tail.

____

5. The cat ran. The cat climbed.

____

Copyright 2006 Growing With Grammar Level 4. All Rights Reserved

C. Underline the **complete predicate** in each sentence. (1.1)

1. The car turned left.
2. Several children went to the mall.
3. Three very hungry boys ate.
4. Chad knocked on the door.
5. The dog jumped.
6. Mary collects butterflies.

D. **Diagram** these sentences. (1.7)

1. Susan bought and wrapped the gift.
2. Terry and Tom live near the store.
3. Bob and Fay forgot their coats.
4. The wind blows or howls.

Copyright 2006 Growing With Grammar Level 4. All Rights Reserved

Worksheet 1.9 (Two Subjects and Two Predicates) Name____________________________

A. Underline each **simple subject** with one line and each **simple predicate** with two lines. **(1.9)**

1. Oscar and Max dusted and vacuumed the house.
2. The horses and donkeys run and kick.
3. Flora and Ella played in the park and flew kites.
4. Magda and her sister ate grapes and drank water.
5. Anna and I laughed and cried during the movie.
6. The boys and girls read and study.
7. The man and dog walked and ran around the block.
8. Barbara and Don baked bread and cooked spaghetti.

B. **Diagram** the simple subjects and simple predicates in these sentences. **(1.4, 1.6, 1.7, & 1.9)**

1. We drove to Seattle.
2. The squid squirted ink.
3. The horses and donkeys run and kick.
4. The tree bent and swayed.
5. Truman and I sang songs.
6. The boys and girls read and study.

Copyright 2006 Growing With Grammar Level 4. All Rights Reserved

C. Draw a line dividing the **complete subject** from the **complete predicate** in these sentences. Decide whether each sentence has a **compound subject** or a **compound predicate**. Write **CS** for compound subject, write **CP** for compound predicate, or write **BOTH** if the sentence has both. **(1.5 & 1.9)**

1. Taylor and Jessica drew pictures. ________________
2. The boys and girls sing and dance. ________________
3. Bees and butterflies carry pollen. ________________
4. The sun rises and sets every day. ________________
5. A runner stopped and rested on the curb. ________________
6. Gavin and Blaire jumped over the fence. ________________
7. Dan and Joe watch movies and play games. ________________
8. Tom and I hugged and kissed Grandma Ruth. ________________

D. **Combine** these sentences to form either a **compound subject** or a **compound predicate**. **(1.8)** (Use the conjunction **or** in at least one sentence.)

1. Dad worked in the garden. Mom worked in the garden.

____

2. The kitten scratched. The kitten clawed.

____

3. Ty scrambled eggs. Ty made toast.

____

4. The cookies are tasty. The brownies are tasty.

____

5. Kayla stubbed her toe. Kayla fell.

____

Copyright 2006 Growing With Grammar Level 4. All Rights Reserved

Worksheet 1.10 (Run-on Sentences) Name____________________________

A. Correct these **run-on sentences** by rewriting them as two separate sentences. **(1.10)**

1. I love to read my sister has a cold.

____

2. Mercury is the closest planet to the sun it is very hot.

____

3. Glenna is a great dancer she practices every day.

____

4. We won the game the score was close.

____

5. It rained all week there was a flood.

____

B. Correct these **run-on sentences** by changing them into **compound sentences** using a **coordinating conjunction**. **(1.10)**

1. Jerry lives around the corner he is my best friend.

____

2. A rainbow formed after the storm it disappeared fast.

____

3. My sister went to the movie I stayed home.

____

4. We played basketball Charlie won.

____

5. He ate all the cake I think he was full.

____

Copyright 2006 Growing With Grammar Level 4. All Rights Reserved

C. Underline each **simple subject** with one line and each **simple predicate** with two lines. **(1.2, 1.3, & 1.9)**

1. Mary and Emma raked the leaves and shoveled the dirt.
2. Troy and I ran home and watched a movie.
3. The wasp and bee buzzed around us and flew away.
4. Al and Paul yelled and screamed at the umpire.
5. Jeremy and Tina sang and danced.

D. **Diagram** the simple subjects and simple predicates in these sentences. **(1.4, 1.6, 1.7, & 1.9)**

1. Bailey opened the door.
2. The boy rode his bike.
3. Bears and lions hunt and rest.
4. The ball bounced and rolled.
5. Chipmunks and squirrels run.
6. Ari and Thora laugh and play.

Copyright 2006 Growing With Grammar Level 4. All Rights Reserved

Worksheet 1.11 (Statements and Questions) Name____________________________

A. In the blank before each sentence, write **S** for **statement** and **Q** for **question**. Place the correct punctuation at the end of each sentence. **(1.11)**

1. ______ Are you finished with your book report___
2. ______ Did Drew hit his head on the table___
3. ______ We visited the museum today___
4. ______ Will you help feed the birds___
5. ______ I like to read stories about brave people in history___
6. ______ James built a snowman in the front yard___
7. ______ Did you take a picture of the eagle___
8. ______ Can you see the moon___
9. ______ Annabelle rang the doorbell to the house___
10. ______ The boy caught the ball and ran for a touchdown___
11. ______ My very hungry brother ate___
12. ______ Did he slide down the pole___
13. ______ Has the band marched onto the field___
14. ______ The man held the door open for his friends___
15. ______ Jeremy sat on the bench___
16. ______ Many birds flew south___
17. ______ Did the tree limb break___
18. ______ Were you having a good time___

Copyright 2006 Growing With Grammar Level 4. All Rights Reserved

B. Rewrite each sentence with correct punctuation and capitalization. **(1.11)**

1. did you study for your test

____

2. i saved some dessert for my sister

____

3. peter hurt his knee

____

4. are you feeling well

____

C. Write a **statement** about yourself. **(1.11)**

____

____

D. Write a **question** about your friend. **(1.11)**

____

____

E. Correct these **run-on sentences** by changing them into **compound sentences** using a conjunction. **(1.10)**

1. Butterflies fly during the day moths mostly fly at night.

____

2. I thought I was late I was wrong.

____

3. David likes to play chess with his brother he always loses.

____

4. Insects have six legs spiders have eight.

____

Copyright 2006 Growing With Grammar Level 4. All Rights Reserved

Worksheet 1.12 (Diagramming Questions) Name____________________________

A. Diagram these **questions**. **(1.12)**

1. Did Thomas eat?

2. Are you singing?

3. Did Gary hide?

4. Can you wait?

5. Is she leaving?

6. Did she clean?

7. Was it raining?

8. Is Bob jogging?

Copyright 2006 Growing With Grammar Level 4. All Rights Reserved

B. In the blank before each sentence, write **S** for **statement** and **Q** for **question**. Place the correct punctuation at the end of each sentence. **(1.11)**

1. _____ Did you vacuum the carpet___
2. _____ Aunt Robyn rode a camel___
3. _____ Is the fan turned on___
4. _____ The volcano erupted___
5. _____ Shayla saw a mountain lion___
6. _____ George plays the guitar___
7. _____ What is the title of your book___
8. _____ Is that a hummingbird___

C. **Combine** these sentences into one sentence to form either a **compound subject** or a **compound predicate**. **(1.8)**

1. Diane danced at the wedding. Her sister danced at the wedding.

____

2. Maria played in the sand. Josh played in the sand.

____

3. Marcus worked hard. Marcus cleaned the basement.

____

4. Many people cheered. Many people clapped.

____

5. The clowns made balloon animals. The clowns performed routines.

____

6. Jacob ate chocolate cake. Emily ate chocolate cake.

____

Copyright 2006 Growing With Grammar Level 4. All Rights Reserved

Worksheet 1.13 (Commands and Exclamations) Name_____________________________

A. Each sentence that follows is either a **command** or an **exclamation**. Identify which is which. Write **C** for **command** and **E** for **exclamation**. Add the correct punctuation at the end of each sentence. **(1.13)**

1. _____ You won the game___
2. _____ Put this away___
3. _____ Take this___
4. _____ The desert is so hot___
5. _____ Stay there___
6. _____ She broke my necklace___
7. _____ I am so angry___
8. _____ Sit down___

B. Write the **subject** of each sentence on the line. Write **(you)** if the subject is **understood**. **(1.13)**

1. ____________________________ Close the window.
2. ____________________________ The pilot waved at us.
3. ____________________________ Be prepared.
4. ____________________________ Find your shoes.
5. ____________________________ The children jumped rope.
6. ____________________________ Randy found a dollar.
7. ____________________________ Wear your hat.
8. ____________________________ Take a picture.
9. ____________________________ You hide.
10. ____________________________ Go home.

Copyright 2006 Growing With Grammar Level 4. All Rights Reserved

C. Underline each **simple subject** with one line and each **simple predicate** with two lines. **(1.9)**

1. Men and women live and travel with the circus.
2. Friends and family danced in a circle and sang songs.
3. Jared and his brother walked to the store and purchased food.
4. Fatima and Rami chased and caught a butterfly.

D. Correct these **run-on sentences** by changing them into **compound sentences** using a conjunction. **(1.10)**

1. Adrian grows tomatoes his mother sells them at the market.

____

2. Blair loves cats she is allergic to them.

____

E. **Diagram** the simple subjects and simple predicates in these sentences. **(1.4, 1.9, & 1.12)**

1. Did Doug eat?
2. Is Chloe making pizza?
3. The book is heavy.
4. Seth and Levi raced home and slept.

Copyright 2006 Growing With Grammar Level 4. All Rights Reserved

Worksheet 1.14 (Diagramming Commands) Name________________________

A. Diagram these **commands**. **(1.14)**

1. Drop the ball.

2. Eat that banana.

3. Help me!

4. Stop!

5. Smile!

6. Feed the dog.

7. Read your book.

8. Go home.

Copyright 2006 Growing With Grammar Level 4. All Rights Reserved

B. Each sentence that follows is a **command**, **exclamation**, or **question**. Identify which is which. Write **C** for **command**, **E** for **exclamation**, or **Q** for question. Add the correct punctuation at the end of each sentence. **(1.11 & 1.13)**

1. _____ Drink plenty of water___
2. _____ Watch out for that snake___
3. _____ Have you seen my keys___
4. _____ I love to fly in jet airplanes___
5. _____ Close the door___
6. _____ Do you want an apple___
7. _____ Did she fasten her seatbelt___
8. _____ That milk is sour___

C. Rewrite each sentence. Change each **question** into a **statement**. **(1.11)**

1. Are you ready to leave?

____

2. Was she tired?

____

3. Is the bag brown?

____

4. Has the team won?

____

D. Change these **fragments** into complete sentences by adding either a **complete subject** or a **complete predicate**. **(1.1)**

1. Kicked the ball.

____

2. This birthday card.

____

3. Was red and black.

____

4. Barry's ball glove.

____

5. Played in the sand.

____

Copyright 2006 Growing With Grammar Level 4. All Rights Reserved

Worksheet 1.15 (Direct Quotations) Name_____________________________

A. Add **quotation marks** to these sentences. Underline the **speaker tags**. **(1.15)**

1. Peter asked, Where are you going?
2. Keith said, I like apple pie.
3. That is a huge ship! exclaimed Carmen.
4. I said, I want to be a doctor.
5. What is bothering you? asked Chiko.
6. Mother yelled, Be careful!
7. Ben said, Have a great day.
8. How are you feeling? asked Rebecca.
9. My uncle is a farmer, said Connor.
10. Andy asked, Is the post office open today?
11. Close the door when you leave, said Dad.
12. Is the shovel in the garage? asked Tyler.
13. I saw a bear! exclaimed Becky.
14. Edith asked, Did you finish your work?
15. Please feed the dog, said Celine.
16. Mary exclaimed, Be careful!
17. The lake is very deep, said Robert.
18. Helen asked, Do you live in England?
19. Michaela said, That actress is my sister.
20. Does that store sell flowers? asked Daryl.

Copyright 2006 Growing With Grammar Level 4. All Rights Reserved

B. Rewrite these **direct quotations**, adding the correct end punctuation, commas, and quotation marks. **(1.15)**

1. Mario said Let's play tag

____

2. Did you take a nap asked Dad

____

3. Amanda yelled I saw a mouse

____

4. I need a snack said George

____

5. Carla asked Did you go fishing

____

6. We are driving to Texas said Samuel

____

7. Have you seen my bike asked Nelson

____

8. I took my money to the bank said Gregory

____

9. Kyle asked How long will the trip take

____

10. Did you see the acrobat fly through the air asked Ty

____

11. Jeremy said My bike is fast

____

12. You broke the window exclaimed John

____

Copyright 2006 Growing With Grammar Level 4. All Rights Reserved

Worksheet 1.16 (Indirect Quotations) Name____________________________

A. Change these direct quotations to **indirect quotations**. **(1.16)**

1. "Rich is taking piano lessons," said Chris.

____

2. Carley said, "The ball went over the fence."

____

3. "Is Missy allergic to cats?" asked Harry.

____

4. "My birthday is in April," said Gina.

____

5. Helen said, "I want to be a doctor."

____

6. "Steve joined the basketball team," said Dan.

____

7. "The runner stole second base," said Clark.

____

8. Mom said, "I saw Mrs. Martin at the grocery store."

____

B. Indicate whether each sentence has a **direct quotation** or an **indirect quotation**. Write **D** for direct and **I** for indirect. Add quotation marks where needed. **(1.15 & 1.16)**

1. _____ Let's play golf, said Jeff.
2. _____ Clark said that Joe went fishing.
3. _____ Todd said that he found a skunk.
4. _____ May I eat? asked Kim.
5. _____ Jason yelled, I'm lost!
6. _____ David said that he is in the play.
7. _____ Mom said, Take this.
8. _____ Is that new? asked Mia.
9. _____ Pat said that he raked the grass.
10. _____ Mia said that she wrote a poem.

Copyright 2006 Growing With Grammar Level 4. All Rights Reserved

C. Underline each **simple subject** with one line and each **simple predicate** with two lines. **(1.2, 1.3, & 1.9)**

1. Myra and Ed made juice and baked brownies.
2. The boys and girls rode bicycles and played catch.
3. Nina and Ryan searched the yard and found the ball.
4. Connor and Herman read and studied.
5. The lions and tigers hunted and ate prey.
6. My aunt and uncle sang and danced in a musical.

D. **Diagram** the simple subjects and simple predicates in these sentences. **(1.4, 1.6, 1.9, 1.12, & 1.14)**

1. The astronaut flew to the moon.
2. Kurt and Ken jumped and yelled.
3. Paul cleaned the basement.
4. Is Jesse sleeping?
5. Did you sing all night?
6. You or Ben help me.
7. Mom and Dad danced in the kitchen.
8. Sharpen the pencil.

Copyright 2006 Growing With Grammar Level 4. All Rights Reserved

Worksheet 1.17(Writing a Paragraph) Name______________________

A. Underline the **topic sentence** in this **paragraph**. Draw a line through the sentence that does not belong. (1.17)

My favorite piece of clothing is my red and blue sweater. It is made with very soft yarn. It fits me perfectly. I love to eat nachos and cheese. The blue color of the sweater matches my eyes. The main reason that it is my favorite piece of clothing is because my Mom made it for me.

B. Below are four **topic sentences**. Write a **paragraph** about one of these sentences. Be sure to make the topic sentence you choose the first sentence of your paragraph. Write two or three more sentences that include specific details about your topic. (1.17)

1. My favorite vacation spot is____________________.
2. The monitor lizard is an interesting animal.
3. ____________________ is my favorite television show.
4. I have an interesting hobby.

____

____

____

____

____

____

____

____

____

____

____

____

____

Copyright 2006 Growing With Grammar Level 4. All Rights Reserved

C. Add **quotation marks**, commas, and end punctuation where needed in these sentences. **(1.15)**

1. Do you have any pets? asked Jerome
2. The band marched onto the field, said Paula
3. The dentist exclaimed, You have a cavity
4. Marissa asked, Have you seen my bracelet
5. I got a yellow bike for my birthday! yelled Elaine
6. Enrique said, I know a great joke
7. Have you ever been to New York? asked Frederick
8. We won the game! exclaimed Kelly

D. Identify whether each group of words is a **fragment**, **sentence**, or **run-on**. Write **F** for fragment, **S** for sentence, or **R** for run-on. **(1.1 & 1.10)**

1. _____ As quiet as mice.
2. _____ Was changed to Tuesday.
3. _____ The microphone was not working I sang anyway.
4. _____ The banana.
5. _____ A jet landed at the airport.
6. _____ Filled the car with gas.
7. _____ Bryan caught the basketball he shot it into the basket.
8. _____ In our backyard.
9. _____ Thomas smiled as he unwrapped the present.
10. _____ A pair of socks.

Copyright 2006 Growing With Grammar Level 4. All Rights Reserved

Chapter 1 Review

Name_______________________________

A. In each sentence, draw a line to divide the **complete subject** from the **complete predicate**. Write the **simple subject** and **simple predicate** on the lines. **(1.1, 1.2, & 1.3)**

1. Tori lost her glasses. ***subject***_______________ ***predicate***________________
2. The red crab pinched me. ***subject***_______________ ***predicate***________________
3. Many people eat sushi. ***subject***_______________ ***predicate***________________
4. The donkey kicks. ***subject***_______________ ***predicate***________________
5. We smiled at the camera. ***subject***_______________ ***predicate***________________
6. Philip ran. ***subject***_______________ ***predicate***________________

B. Decide if each group of words is a complete **sentence** or a **fragment**. Write F for fragment or **S** for sentence. **(1.1)**

1. ______ Is laughing.
2. ______ Makina planted a tree.
3. ______ Warren's tooth is loose.
4. ______ A baby tiger.
5. ______ Frances collects butterflies.
6. ______ Found a dime and a book.

C. **Combine** each pair of these sentences into one sentence to include either a **compound subject** or a **compound predicate**. **(1.8)**

1. Fruits are part of a healthy diet. Vegetables are part of a healthy diet.

____

2. The coach watched. The coach offered suggestions.

____

3. The girls entered the room. The girls sat on the bench.

____

4. Gage wore sunglasses. Bess wore sunglasses.

____

Copyright 2006 Growing With Grammar Level 4. All Rights Reserved

D. Correct these **run-on sentences** by changing them into **compound sentences** using a conjunction. **(1.10)**

1. My sister won the race she was happy.

____

2. The movie started on time we were late.

____

E. Identify whether each sentence is a **command**, **exclamation**, or **question**. Write **C** for **command**, **E** for **exclamation**, or **Q** for question. Add the correct punctuation at the end of each sentence. **(1.11 & 1.13)**

1. _____ I am so upset___
2. _____ Did you break the dish___
3. _____ Leave your shoes on the porch___
4. _____ Is that your house___
5. _____ We won___
6. _____ The water is too cold___
7. _____ Have you been sleeping___
8. _____ Rake the leaves___

F. Write whether each sentence has a **direct quotation** or an **indirect quotation**. Write **D** for direct or **I** for indirect. Add quotation marks where needed. **(1.15 & 1.16)**

1. _____ Louisa said that her father went to Paris.
2. _____ We are leaving in fifteen minutes, said Sylvia.
3. _____ Audrey said that she is feeling better today.
4. _____ Danny asked if we would arrive on time.
5. _____ Have you seen my new gloves? asked Gene.
6. _____ Sandra said that she will be flying to Hawaii.
7. _____ Nancy exclaimed, I think it's going to storm!
8. _____ Skylar asked, Is Jamie coming to the party?

Copyright 2006 Growing With Grammar Level 4. All Rights Reserved

G. **Diagram** the simple subjects and simple predicates in these sentences.
(1.4, 1.6, 1.7, 1.9, 1.12, & 1.14)

1. Martha lost a tooth.

2. Joey climbs and explores.

3. Take this.

4. Did you read this book?

5. Mary and Josie played a game.

6. Can you wait?

7. Jade and Brett sat down and ate dinner.

8. You and Gary paint the house.

Copyright 2006 Growing With Grammar Level 4. All Rights Reserved

Copyright 2006 Growing With Grammar Level 4. All Rights Reserved

Worksheet 2.1 (Common Nouns and Proper Nouns) Name________________________

A. Underline all the **nouns** in each sentence. **(2.1)**

1. A small monkey sat in the tree.
2. The woman opened the door.
3. The bracelet was made of noodles.
4. Marian bought a bike at the store.
5. My family hiked in the canyon.
6. Amanda sat on the bench.
7. The child ran across the street.
8. Amy used apples for the pie.

B. Write a **proper noun** for each **common noun** listed below. **(2.1)**

1. city ____________________
2. river ____________________
3. girl ____________________
4. state ____________________
5. day ____________________
6. ocean ____________________
7. store ____________________
8. continent ____________________
9. artist ____________________
10. queen ____________________
11. neighbor ____________________
12. holiday ____________________
13. explorer ____________________
14. mountain ____________________

C. On the line after each **noun**, write whether it is a **person**, **place**, or **thing**. **(2.1)**

1. clown ____________
2. sock ____________
3. neighbor ____________
4. zoo ____________
5. friend ____________
6. rock ____________
7. beach ____________
8. knife ____________

Copyright 2006 Growing With Grammar Level 4. All Rights Reserved

D. Find the **proper nouns** in each sentence. Write them correctly on the line. **(2.1)**

1. robby visited europe last year.

____

2. My sister was born on a friday in september.

____

3. My favorite president is abraham lincoln.

____

4. On monday we leave for arizona.

____

5. tim could see the atlantic ocean from his window.

____

6. joseph misses his friend martin.

____

E. Decide if these nouns are **proper nouns** or **common nouns**. Write **P** for proper or **C** for common. **(2.1)**

1. _____ seat
2. _____ Massachusetts
3. _____ January
4. _____ book
5. _____ Washington Monument
6. _____ holiday
7. _____ street
8. _____ day
9. _____ Canada
10. _____ Anna
11. _____ king
12. _____ Europe
13. _____ Lincoln Zoo
14. _____ Boston
15. _____ lake
16. _____ Italy
17. _____ girl
18. _____ sea
19. _____ Pacific Ocean
20. _____ college

Copyright 2006 Growing With Grammar Level 4. All Rights Reserved

Worksheet 2.2 (Concrete and Abstract Nouns) Name______________________________

A. Decide if these nouns are **concrete nouns** or **abstract nouns**. Write **C** for **concrete** or **A** for **abstract**. **(2.2)**

1. ______ floor
2. ______ truth
3. ______ joy
4. ______ clock
5. ______ China
6. ______ patience
7. ______ farmer
8. ______ love
9. ______ honesty
10. ______ cat
11. ______ dog
12. ______ book
13. ______ friend
14. ______ doctor
15. ______ kindness
16. ______ baseball
17. ______ success
18. ______ loyalty
19. ______ food
20. ______ flower
21. ______ wisdom
22. ______ honor
23. ______ truck
24. ______ thought
25. ______ football
26. ______ hope
27. ______ apple
28. ______ restaurant
29. ______ loneliness
30. ______ river
31. ______ paper
32. ______ bravery
33. ______ town
34. ______ kitchen
35. ______ sister
36. ______ goodness
37. ______ time
38. ______ bowl
39. ______ fan
40. ______ blanket

Copyright 2006 Growing With Grammar Level 4. All Rights Reserved

B. Underline the **abstract nouns** in these sentences. **(2.2)**

1. Mick finished his work early.
2. It took great courage to hold the snake.
3. Grandfather never breaks his promises.
4. The excitement of the puppy made us laugh.

C. Complete each sentence with a **noun**. **(2.1 & 2.2)**

1. ______________________________ are my favorite vegetables.
2. The ______________________________ was bright in the night sky.
3. Place the _________________________ near the _____________________________.
4. Chipmunks eat ______________________________.
5. Can you catch a ______________________________?
6. ______________________________ are my favorite kind of animal.
7. The ______________________________ must be mowed.
8. Do you like to drink ______________________________?

D. **Diagram** the simple subjects and simple predicates in these sentences.
(1.4, 1.6, 1.7, 1.9, 1.12, & 1.14)

1. Read this book.
2. Jeff played an instrument and sang.
3. Do you play music?
4. Janet and Ted laughed at the joke.
5. Mom answered my question.
6. Anika and Claire sat and talked.

Copyright 2006 Growing With Grammar Level 4. All Rights Reserved

Worksheet 2.3 (Compound Nouns) Name____________________________

A. Write the nouns that make up each **compound noun**. (2.3)

1. sunlight ____________________
2. mailbox ____________________
3. keyboard ____________________
4. lighthouse ____________________
5. motorcycle ____________________
6. seatbelt ____________________
7. drugstore ____________________
8. bedroom ____________________
9. flowerpot ____________________
10. bookcase ____________________
11. drive-in ____________________
12. merry-go-round ____________________
13. hide-and-seek ____________________
14. babysitter ____________________

B. Write a **compound noun** for these phrases. (2.3)

1. a pot for flowers ____________________
2. light from the sun ____________________
3. a washer for the dishes ____________________
4. a line for clothes ____________________
5. a house for a dog ____________________
6. a room for the bath ____________________

Copyright 2006 Growing With Grammar Level 4. All Rights Reserved

C. In each sentence, underline the **compound nouns**. **(2.3)**

1. We stopped at the post office to mail our letters.
2. I loaded the dishwasher with the dirty dishes.
3. Allan got a fish tank when he turned nine.
4. My brother dropped his toothbrush on the floor.
5. Mom is fixing meatloaf for dinner and ice cream for desert.
6. The policeman caught the thief.
7. They purchased their tickets from the ticket agent.
8. Mieko hit the tennis ball over the net.
9. A yellow butterfly landed on a sunflower.
10. Dan read the newspaper while he listened to the football game.
11. Joey received a jack-in-the-box and a toy airplane as gifts.
12. Will you look in the bathroom for the toothpaste?
13. I put my softball into my backpack as I walked to the ballpark.
14. There was a full moon as we played basketball last night.
15. Kate can do a handstand in the swimming pool.
16. Our dog hid in the doghouse during the thunderstorm.

D. Write two sentences about a country you would like to visit. Use as many **proper nouns** as you can and underline them. **(2.1)**

____

____

____

____

____

Copyright 2006 Growing With Grammar Level 4. All Rights Reserved

Worksheet 2.4 (Plural Nouns) Name____________________________

A. Write the **plural form** of each **noun**. **(2.4)**

1. stitch ____________________________
2. hat ____________________________
3. brush ____________________________
4. star ____________________________
5. fox ____________________________
6. storm ____________________________
7. dress ____________________________
8. paper ____________________________
9. glass ____________________________
10. fork ____________________________
11. beach ____________________________
12. farm ____________________________
13. owner ____________________________
14. mix ____________________________
15. horse ____________________________
16. mess ____________________________

B. Make these **nouns plural** by adding **<u>s</u>** or **<u>es</u>** to the end of the word. **(2.4)**

1. cello_________
2. hero_________
3. stereo_________
4. banjo_________
5. rodeo_________
6. potato_________
7. solo_________
8. studio_________
9. piano_________
10. soprano_________
11. tomato_________
12. patio_________
13. mosquito_________
14. echo_________
15. yo-yo_________
16. radio_________
17. alto_________
18. cameo_________

Copyright 2006 Growing With Grammar Level 4. All Rights Reserved

C. Complete each sentence with a plural noun. **(2.4)**

1. ____________________________ are hard workers.
2. There are different kinds of ____________________________.
3. An atlas has ____________________________.
4. My mother owns several ____________________________.
5. The ____________________________ are red and juicy.
6. We planted ____________________________ in our garden.
7. The ____________________________ are growing.
8. ____________________________ have feathers.

D. Rewrite these **sentences** using proper punctuation and capitalization. **(1.10, 1.11, & 2.1)**

1. troy set his alarm but he was late for practice

____

2. will you pass the potatoes

____

3. have you seen the pacific ocean

____

4. my friend jared lives in idaho

____

5. we went to the movies but sally stayed home

____

6. jack dropped the vase

____

Copyright 2006 Growing With Grammar Level 4. All Rights Reserved

Worksheet 2.5 (More Plural Nouns) Name______________________________

A. Write the **plural form** of each **noun**. **(2.5)**

1. penny ______________________
2. fly ______________________
3. loaf ______________________
4. baby ______________________
5. essay ______________________
6. wolf ______________________
7. thief ______________________
8. guy ______________________
9. toy ______________________
10. valley ______________________
11. monkey ______________________
12. shelf ______________________
13. army ______________________
14. knife ______________________
15. lady ______________________
16. cherry ______________________

B. Mark an X next to the **plural nouns** that are spelled correctly. **(2.5)**

1. ________beautys
2. ________turkeys
3. ________dayes
4. ________wifes
5. ________leaves
6. ________familys
7. ________copies
8. ________berries
9. ________cliffs
10. ________chimneies
11. ________ponys
12. ________scarfs
13. ________keys
14. ________halves
15. ________bodys
16. ________countries
17. ________calves
18. ________nannys
19. ________dutys
20. ________donkeys

Copyright 2006 Growing With Grammar Level 4. All Rights Reserved

C. Decide if these nouns are **concrete nouns** or **abstract nouns**. Write **C** for **concrete** or **A** for **abstract**. **(2.2)**

1. _____ time
2. _____ cat
3. _____ computer
4. _____ bravery
5. _____ nose
6. _____ trust
7. _____ bus
8. _____ flag
9. _____ law
10. _____ brother
11. _____ shirt
12. _____ hope
13. _____ love
14. _____ loyalty
15. _____ flower
16. _____ success

D. Write a **proper noun** for each **common noun** listed below. **(2.1)**

1. person ______________________________
2. lake ______________________________
3. president ______________________________
4. man ______________________________
5. holiday ______________________________
6. state ______________________________
7. street ______________________________
8. day ______________________________
9. country ______________________________
10. pet ______________________________

Copyright 2006 Growing With Grammar Level 4. All Rights Reserved

Worksheet 2.6 (Irregular Plural Nouns) Name________________________

A. Write the **plural form** of these nouns. **(2.6)**

1. woman________________________
2. scissors________________________
3. goose ________________________
4. bison ________________________
5. pliers ________________________
6. man ________________________
7. ox ________________________
8. deer ________________________
9. sheep ________________________
10. salmon ________________________
11. foot ________________________
12. person ________________________
13. glasses ________________________
14. moose ________________________
15. trout ________________________
16. mouse ________________________

B. Write the **plural form** of each **noun**. **(2.4, 2.5, & 2.6)**

1. day ________________________
2. leaf ________________________
3. roof ________________________
4. stereo ________________________
5. cameo ________________________
6. mix ________________________
7. buggy ________________________
8. key ________________________
9. potato ________________________
10. rodeo ________________________

C. Indicate whether the **noun** in bold is **singular** or **plural** in each sentence. Write **S** for singular or **P** for plural. **(2.6)**

1. ______ I love that pair of **pants**.
2. ______ Jodi lost two **teeth** last night.
3. ______ A **moose** was standing in our driveway.
4. ______ Those **women** have been standing in line for an hour.
5. ______ The **people** cheered for the football team.
6. ______ Is that a **goose** flying overhead?

Copyright 2006 Growing With Grammar Level 4. All Rights Reserved

D. Think about walking through the forest. Write two to three sentences describing what you might see using **irregular plural nouns**. Circle the **nouns**. **(2.6)**

____

____

____

____

____

____

____

E. **Diagram** the simple subjects and simple predicates in these sentences. **(1.4, 1.6, 1.7, 1.9, 1.12, & 1.14)**

1. The deer jumped the fence.
2. The men and women ate cherries.
3. Did you see the geese?
4. I found pliers and fixed my glasses.
5. Brush the pony.
6. Tomatoes and potatoes thrive and grow.

Copyright 2006 Growing With Grammar Level 4. All Rights Reserved

Worksheet 2.7 (Singular Possessive Nouns) Name________________________

A. Rewrite each group of words using the **possessive** form for each **noun**. **(2.7)**

1. a birthday of a friend ________________________
2. the chair belonging to the boss ________________________
3. the order of the customer ________________________
4. a claw belonging to a crab ________________________
5. the script owned by the actress ________________________
6. the propeller of the boat ________________________
7. the knife belonging to the cook ________________________
8. the cough that James has ________________________
9. the car owned by the driver ________________________
10. the hoot of the owl ________________________
11. the mitt of the cook ________________________
12. the jacket of the woman ________________________
13. the hive of the bee ________________________
14. the stripes of the zebra ________________________
15. the decision of your Mom ________________________
16. the toys of the boy ________________________

B. Circle the correct word for each sentence. Write on the line if the noun is **plural** or **possessive**. **(2.4, 2.5, & 2.7)**

1. Your (cats, cat's) eyes are different colors. ________________
2. The (trees, tree's) were swaying in the wind. ________________
3. Is that (Davids, David's) bicycle? ________________
4. (Kathys, Kathy's) painting is beautiful. ________________

Copyright 2006 Growing With Grammar Level 4. All Rights Reserved

C. Write the **plural** form of each **noun**. **(2.6)**

1. goose ______________________
2. pants ______________________
3. swine ______________________
4. person ______________________
5. child ______________________
6. tooth ______________________
7. pliers ______________________
8. moose ______________________

D. Decide if the **noun** is bold is **singular** or **plural** in these sentences. Write **S** for singular and **P** for plural. **(2.6)**

1. _____ We saw three **deer** in the field.
2. _____ Grandpa caught one **trout** when he went fishing.
3. _____ Joe lost two **teeth** yesterday.
4. _____ The **woman** waved at us.

E. Put these sentences in correct order to form a **paragraph**. **(1.17)**

After the show, we went to see the lions.

Our trip to the zoo was fun.

Next we watched the dolphin show.

Finally we watched the elephants play in their pond.

First we saw the seals and walruses.

____

____

____

____

____

____

____

____

____

____

Copyright 2006 Growing With Grammar Level 4. All Rights Reserved

Worksheet 2.8 (Plural Possessive Nouns) Name____________________________

A. Write the **possessive** form of each **plural noun**. **(2.8)**

1. boys ____________________
2. men ____________________
3. geese ____________________
4. farmers ____________________
5. children ____________________
6. students ____________________
7. horses ____________________
8. mice ____________________
9. women ____________________
10. ladies ____________________

B. Rewrite these phrases by using the **possessive** form of each **plural noun** in bold. **(2.8)**

1. the paintings of the **artists** ______________________________
2. the helmets owned by **astronauts** ______________________________
3. the keys belonging to the **people** ______________________________
4. the fields belonging to the **farmers** ______________________________
5. the friends of the **children** ______________________________
6. the tails of the **dogs** ______________________________

C. Write the **possessive** form of each **noun**. **(2.7 & 2.8)**

1. a plant ____________________
2. the bees ____________________
3. James ____________________
4. a waitress ____________________
5. Clara ____________________
6. the friends ____________________
7. a goose ____________________
8. the class ____________________

Copyright 2006 Growing With Grammar Level 4. All Rights Reserved

D. Circle the correct **noun** for each sentence. Write on the line if the **possessive noun** is **singular** or **plural**. **(2.7 & 2.8)**

1. The (fishermen's, fishermens') nets catch many fish. ________________________
2. My (sisters, sister's) shoes are blue. ________________________
3. (Moms', Mom's) coat is on the couch. ________________________
4. This (turtle's, turtles') shell is spotted. ________________________
5. There are many (bird's, birds') nests in the tree. ________________________
6. The cat stole the (mice's, mices) cheese. ________________________
7. The (childrens', children's) bikes were in the yard. ________________________
8. The (waitresses, waitress's) pencil fell on the floor. ________________________
9. The (peoples, people's) opinions were strong. ________________________
10. Hudson knows how to work on a (cars, car's) engine. ________________________
11. (James', James's) sister won first prize. ________________________
12. We went to my (uncles, uncle's) house. ________________________
13. That (butterflys, butterfly's) wings are blue and gold. ________________________
14. Is this (Amandas, Amanda's) glove? ________________________

E. Rewrite these sentences using proper **capitalization** and **punctuation**. **(1.10, 1.11, & 2.1)**

1. i do not like vanilla but I love chocolate

____

2. did tommy arrive yet

____

3. my sister goes to the library on tuesday

____

4. the doorbell rang and jordan answered the door

____

Copyright 2006 Growing With Grammar Level 4. All Rights Reserved

Worksheet 2.9 (Nouns of Direct Address) Name___________________________

A. Add the missing commas to these sentences with **nouns of direct address**. **(2.9)**

1. Where are we going Angie?
2. I think Devin that you have won.
3. Andrew you are a great friend.
4. Madison did you feed the horses?
5. Yes Caroline I went to the dentist.
6. I am leaving with my friends Mom.
7. Should I bring my lunch Mark?
8. No Alice we are not moving.
9. To be honest Dean I do not know.
10. Kim pass me the potatoes.
11. Sit next to me Emmett.
12. Next week Dad I am going to camp.
13. Jay are you feeling well?
14. Your shoe is untied Henry.
15. Mandy you have a great singing voice.
16. Dan I lost my glasses at the park.
17. Yes Melanie you may try again.
18. Do you need a ride Austin?

B. Use the names of your family members to write two sentences showing different types of **direct address**. **(2.9)**

1. ____

____

2. ____

____

Copyright 2006 Growing With Grammar Level 4. All Rights Reserved

C. Write a **proper noun** for each **common noun** listed below. **(2.1)**

1. city ______________________ 4. holiday ______________________

2. woman ______________________ 5. ocean ______________________

3. desert ______________________ 6. state ______________________

D. Rewrite these **quotations** adding capital letters, commas, quotation marks, and end punctuation. **(1.5)**

1. dad said clean under your bed

____

2. where is my pillow asked kate

____

3. i lost my purse exclaimed shelly

____

4. grandpa asked are you coming for dinner

____

E. Underline the **topic sentence** in this **paragraph** and cross out any sentence that does not belong. **(1.17)**

In every season, there is something fun for children to do. Spring is a good time to fly kites and plant flowers. I love thunderstorms. Summer is a good time to swim and have picnics. Fall is when we play in the leaves and pick pumpkins. Winter is the time to make snowmen and go sledding.

Copyright 2006 Growing With Grammar Level 4. All Rights Reserved

Worksheet 2.10 (Noun Suffixes) Name______________________________

A. Write the correct word for each meaning below by using the word in bold as a base word and adding a **noun suffix**. **(2.10)**

1. someone who **fight**s ______________________________
2. someone who **drive**s ______________________________
3. someone who **paint**s ______________________________
4. someone who **build**s ______________________________
5. someone who is **aggress**ive ______________________________
6. someone who **direct**s ______________________________
7. something that **erase**s ______________________________
8. something that **open**s ______________________________
9. someone who **decorate**s ______________________________
10. someone who **conduct**s ______________________________
11. something that **toast**s ______________________________
12. someone who **visit**s ______________________________
13. someone who **manage**s ______________________________
14. someone who **sail**s ______________________________

B. Write the meaning for each word. **(2.10)**

1. planner______________________________
2. teacher______________________________
3. actor______________________________
4. painter______________________________
5. visitor______________________________
6. camper______________________________

Copyright 2006 Growing With Grammar Level 4. All Rights Reserved

C. Write the **plural form** of these nouns. **(2.6)**

1. key ______________________
2. mouse ______________________
3. fox ______________________
4. army ______________________
5. louse ______________________
6. calf ______________________
7. ash ______________________
8. watch ______________________
9. half ______________________
10. sheep ______________________
11. copy ______________________
12. glasses ______________________

D. **Diagram** the simple subjects and simple predicates in these sentences.
(1.4, 1.6, 1.7, 1.9, 1.12, & 1.14)

1. Can you wait?
2. Has Charlie left?
3. Go home.
4. Did you read this book?
5. Sit down.
6. Take this.

Copyright 2006 Growing With Grammar Level 4. All Rights Reserved

Worksheet 2.11 (Dictionary Skills) Name___________________________

A. Circle each word that would be on a dictionary page with the **guide words** listed in bold. **(2.11)**

1. **moderate – monkey**

   mistake mold moment mulch mollusk murmur

2. **pants – patch**

   partridge peep pint parent paper pad

3. **skim – sliver**

   skull silk slate small shrimp slope

4. **take – tarantula**

   table tail talent talon tantrum tape

5. **kangaroo – kind**

   keen jungle kneel kite key kick

6. **parkway – petticoat**

   pheasant partner pajamas passage peace pelt

7. **football – fruit**

   forceps fountain flute frenzy fuzzy fury

8. **letter – lift**

   lecture leopard library lid load level

B. Write these groups of words in **alphabetical order**. **(2.11)**

1. diamond ______________________	2. fast ______________________
carpet ______________________	film ______________________
blanket ______________________	flavor ______________________
emperor ______________________	festive ______________________
acid ______________________	foal ______________________

Copyright 2006 Growing With Grammar Level 4. All Rights Reserved

3. mistake ______________________ 4. while ______________________

nimble ______________________ weak ______________________

mail ______________________ wheel ______________________

natural ______________________ whale ______________________

modem ______________________ welt ______________________

C. Circle the **correct spelling** of the words in parentheses. Check in the **dictionary** if you are unsure. **(2.11)**

1. Hot is the (opasit, opposite, oposite) of cold.
2. This spaghetti is (delicious, delishous, dalicious).
3. Magda needs to (pratise, practice, pracktise) the piano today.
4. The (capital, capitall, cappital) city of Illinois is Springfield.
5. Mom's porcelain plates are (frajile, fragile, frajule) and should be handled with care.
6. Cameron was (eager, eeger, eagur) to learn about the Revolutionary War.
7. This book has a lot of (informashun, information, enformation) about sports.
8. I need to write a (paragraph, peragraph, paragraf) about my summer vacation.
9. Stella and Shae have a great (friendship, frendship, freindship).
10. Our (naybor, naghbor, neighbor) borrowed the lawn mower.

D. Rewrite these phrases by using the **possessive** form of each **plural noun** in bold. **(2.8)**

1. the computers owned by the **girls** ______________________________
2. the houses belonging to the **people** ______________________________
3. the jackets belonging to the **men** ______________________________
4. the trophies of the **winners** ______________________________
5. the titles of the **books** ______________________________
6. the adventures of the **women** ______________________________

Copyright 2006 Growing With Grammar Level 4. All Rights Reserved

Chapter 2 Review

Name______________________________

A. Underline all the **nouns** in each sentence. **(2.1)**

1. Tammy opened the window.
2. Jimmy threw a ball.
3. The boy caught a fish in the lake.
4. The bird built a nest in the bush.
5. The chef made spaghetti.
6. The lion jumped through the ring.

B. Write a **proper noun** for each **common noun** listed below. **(2.1)**

1. river ______________________________
2. ocean ______________________________
3. boy ______________________________
4. country ______________________________
5. month ______________________________
6. aunt ______________________________
7. street ______________________________
8. explorer ______________________________
9. continent ______________________________
10. president ______________________________

C. Identify whether these nouns are **concrete** or **abstract**. Write **C** for **concrete** or **A** for **abstract**. **(2.2)**

1. _____ hamburger
2. _____ wisdom
3. _____ joy
4. _____ thought
5. _____ car
6. _____ girl
7. _____ truth
8. _____ coat
9. _____ honor
10. _____ dollar

Copyright 2006 Growing With Grammar Level 4. All Rights Reserved

D. Write a **compound noun** for these phrases. **(2.3)**

1. a loaf made of meat ______________________
2. a belt for a seat ______________________
3. a box for mail ______________________
4. a paper containing news ______________________
5. paste that cleans teeth ______________________
6. a room for the bath ______________________

E. Write the **plural form** of each **noun**. **(2.4, 2.5, & 2.6)**

1. soprano ______________
2. glass ______________
3. donkey ______________
4. scissors ______________
5. ball ______________
6. half ______________
7. valley ______________
8. fly ______________
9. pliers ______________
10. woman ______________
11. person ______________
12. sheep ______________
13. hero ______________
14. loaf ______________
15. penny ______________
16. goose ______________
17. bison ______________
18. lunch ______________
19. essay ______________
20. tomato ______________

F. Rewrite each group of words by using the **possessive** form of each **noun** in bold. **(2.7)**

1. the sister of **Bianca** ______________________
2. the cello belonging to **Charles** ______________________
3. the hoot of the **owl** ______________________
4. a shell belonging to **Sally** ______________________
5. the story of the **witness** ______________________

Copyright 2006 Growing With Grammar Level 4. All Rights Reserved

G. Rewrite each group of words by using the **possessive** form of each **plural noun** in bold. **(2.8)**

1. the laws of the **states** ____________________
2. the feathers of the **geese** ____________________
3. the books belonging to the **children** ____________________
4. the boat of the **sailors** ____________________

H. Add the missing commas to these sentences with **nouns of direct address**. **(2.9)**

1. Tiffany where did you go?
2. Yes Bruno the chair is broken.
3. Did you finish your chores Elliot?
4. I thought Polly that you were finished.
5. Andrew you are a great football player.

I. Write the correct word for each meaning below by using the word in bold as a base word and adding a **noun suffix**. **(2.10)**

1. something that **open**s ____________________
2. someone who **race**s ____________________
3. someone who **farm**s ____________________
4. someone who **navigate**s ____________________
5. someone who **decorate**s ____________________

J. Circle each word that would be on a dictionary page with the **guide words** listed in bold. **(2.11)**

1. **water – wheat**

wicker wind wax weather warm wade

2. **invent – it**

ironic iodine ivy iris iron image

Copyright 2006 Growing With Grammar Level 4. All Rights Reserved

K. Write these groups of words in **alphabetical order**. (2.11)

1. juice	______________	2. relax	______________
fancy	______________	ruler	______________
honey	______________	rigid	______________
limit	______________	roof	______________
nature	______________	race	______________

Copyright 2006 Growing With Grammar Level 4. All Rights Reserved

Worksheet 3.1 (Pronouns) Name__________________________

A. Underline the **pronouns** in each sentence. **(3.1)**

1. I waved to them.
2. She gave chocolate chip cookies to him.
3. Is he related to you?
4. They took us to the carnival.
5. We heard her making plans for a surprise party.
6. It frightened me!
7. I asked him for a book.
8. They watched her cat.
9. He is a friend to me.
10. You are going to the park with us.

B. Write a **pronoun** on the lines to take the place of the repeating nouns. **(3.1)**

1. Duane was shouting for Duane's sister until Duane lost Duane's voice.

   Duane was shouting for _________ sister until _________ lost _________ voice.

2. Lilly has the postcard that Lilly's cousin wrote to Lilly.

   Lilly has the postcard that _________cousin wrote to _________.

3. Kim and Sara saw Bob wave at Kim and Sara.

   Kim and Sara saw Bob wave at _________.

4. Stu and I walked home when Stu and I saw a kite that belonged to Stu and me.

   Stu and I were walking home when_________saw a kite that belonged to_________.

Copyright 2006 Growing With Grammar Level 4. All Rights Reserved

C. Write a **pronoun** to replace each of the underlined words in the sentences. Use the pronoun **he**, **she**, **it**, **we**, or **they**. **(3.1)**

1. Cora held up her hand. ____________________
2. The boys ate dinner quickly. ____________________
3. Maria and I are learning Chinese. ____________________
4. I gave a bone to the dog. ____________________
5. Teddy listened to Margaret. ____________________
6. Ned can whistle really well. ____________________
7. Lana and Emily rode with Grace. ____________________
8. A ladybug flew into the house. ____________________

D. Rewrite these sentences using proper capitalization and punctuation. **(1.10, 1.11, & 2.1)**

1. carl thought he saw a snake but it was a lizard

____

2. do feathers keep birds warm

____

E. Decide if these nouns are **proper nouns** or **common nouns**. Write **P** for proper or **C** for common. **(2.1)**

1. _____ motorcycle
2. _____ Iowa
3. _____ lettuce
4. _____ pineapple
5. _____ Wednesday
6. _____ Austria
7. _____ engine
8. _____ London
9. _____ Paul Gauguin
10. _____ May

Copyright 2006 Growing With Grammar Level 4. All Rights Reserved

Worksheet 3.2 (Subject and Object Pronouns) Name______________________

A. Circle the correct **pronoun** for each sentence. **(3.2)**

1. (She, Her) found a shell in the sand.
2. (I, Me) won a trophy.
3. Henry bought (he, him) a book.
4. Jerry asked (we, us) for a ride.
5. (They, Them) ate lunch at home.
6. The duck followed (me, I) to the pond.
7. (I, Me) like to read.
8. (He, Him) likes pancakes.
9. (Them, They) went sledding.
10. The soup is for (we, us).

B. Write a **pronoun** on the line to replace the noun(s) in bold in each sentence. **(3.1 & 3.2)**

1. **Mom and Dad** read the newspaper in the morning. ______________
2. Sherry gave the balloons to **Mark and me**. ______________
3. **Dr. Edgar** is a veterinarian. ______________
4. We are going to visit **Maria** soon. ______________
5. **Jude and I** walked to the store. ______________
6. I like **Daniel** a lot. ______________
7. The bus took **Jennifer and me** to the museum. ______________
8. Annie fed **the dog**. ______________
9. **Sally** made lunch. ______________
10. **My friend and I** read the newspaper. ______________

Copyright 2006 Growing With Grammar Level 4. All Rights Reserved

C. Circle each **pronoun** in these sentences. **(3.1 & 3.2)**

1. Have you ever seen a ballet?
2. We learned about the pyramids.
3. I would like to write a letter to her.
4. She and I want to pass the exam.
5. Did you invite him to the party?
6. Grandma thanked us for helping her.
7. They arrived this afternoon.
8. Roy helped Claudia and me with our work.

D. Write three or four sentences about something fun you do with friends. Circle the **pronouns** in your sentences. **(3.1 & 3.2)**

____

____

____

____

____

____

____

____

____

____

Copyright 2006 Growing With Grammar Level 4. All Rights Reserved

Worksheet 3.3 (Possessive Pronouns) Name_______________________________

A. For each sentence, write a **possessive pronoun** on the line to replace the word in bold. **(3.3)**

1. Today is **Jay's** birthday. Today is ___________ birthday.
2. The **mouse's** tail is long. ___________ tail is long.
3. The book report belongs to **Ana.** The book report is ___________.
4. That is **my** hat. The hat is ___________.
5. Those are **your** earrings. Those earrings are ___________.
6. The house belongs to **Fred and George**. It is___________ house.
7. The watch is **Maria's**. It is ___________ watch .
8. **Roy's** brother is older. ___________ brother is older.

B. Circle the correct **possessive pronoun** for each sentence. **(3.3)**

1. Janie said (hers, her) sweater is too large.
2. Is this (your, yours) dog?
3. We are eating trout for (our, ours) dinner.
4. (Mine, My) uncle lives in Paris.
5. The cat licked (it's, its) paws.
6. Which book is (her's, hers)?
7. Tomas and I talked about (our, ours) trip to Ireland.
8. Selma wrote a report about (her, hers) book.
9. The children had fun playing with (theirs, their) puppy.
10. Malcolm, this hat is (your's, yours).

Copyright 2006 Growing With Grammar Level 4. All Rights Reserved

C. Circle the correct **pronoun** for each sentence. **(3.2 & 3.3)**

1. (We, Us) watched Mrs. Smith's cat while (she, her) was on vacation.
2. (They, Them) walked along the riverbank with (I, me).
3. Daura sat next to (he, him).
4. (He, Him) took an invitation to (they, them).
5. (She, Her) house is near the park.
6. (They, Them) sent postcards to (we, us).

D. **Diagram** the simple subjects and simple predicates in these sentences. **(1.4, 1.6, 1.12, & 1.14)**

1. Manuel and Rosa made dinner for us.
2. Did you hear that song?
3. Help her.
4. Spencer is my brother.

Copyright 2006 Growing With Grammar Level 4. All Rights Reserved

Worksheet 3.4 (Personal Pronouns) Name____________________________

A. On the line after each sentence, write the **antecedent** for the **personal pronoun** in bold. **(3.4)**

*Example: Cody had **his** backpack.* ___*Cody*___

1. Mary, **you** look tired. ____________________
2. "**I** want to go down the slide," said Baxter. ____________________
3. The bird carried food to **its** young. ____________________
4. Jerry drew pictures in **his** notebook. ____________________
5. Is this **your** fishing pole, Alan? ____________________
6. Nico and Omar wrote a letter to **their** cousin. ____________________
7. Sebastian said, "That stamp collection is **mine**." ____________________
8. Trudy said that **she** loves to learn about whales. ____________________
9. **You** are a great soccer player, Ed. ____________________
10. Amber and Maria said that rabbit is **theirs**. ____________________
11. Asta brushes **her** hair. ____________________
12. George and I went to see **our** grandmother. ____________________
13. Caleb wrote a letter to **his** friend. ____________________
14. The rabbit ran for **its** life. ____________________
15. The goslings followed **their** mother. ____________________
16. Stefan, **your** dinner is ready. ____________________
17. Laura cleaned **her** room. ____________________
18. Does **your** printer work, Brad? ____________________
19. Sloane and Kirsten played with **their** puppy. ____________________
20. Ed and I ate **our** lunch quickly. ____________________

Copyright 2006 Growing With Grammar Level 4. All Rights Reserved

B. Complete the following sentences with a **personal pronoun** that refers to the antecedent in bold. **(3.4)**

1. My **sister** wore __________ new dress today.
2. **Craig and Lorna** could not find __________ mother.
3. The **wolf** licked __________ paws.
4. The doctor asked **me** about __________ symptoms.
5. **Dad** is looking forward to __________ vacation.
6. **Conrad** likes to look through __________ telescope.
7. **Missy and Belle** said __________ are going to the game on Friday.
8. **We** painted __________ fence today.

C. Write a **possessive pronoun** on the line to take the place of the possessive noun. **(3.3)**

1. Jane's decision ______________________________
2. the children's sand castle ______________________________
3. the fisherman's bait ______________________________
4. the television's sound ______________________________
5. my family's home ______________________________
6. the house's roof ______________________________
7. the skaters' skates ______________________________
8. Kate's manners ______________________________

D. Write the **plural form** of each **noun**. **(2.4, 2.5, & 2.6)**

1. ash	____________________	5. letter	____________________
2. story	____________________	6. mystery	____________________
3. person	____________________	7. fish	____________________
4. tooth	____________________	8. tray	____________________

Copyright 2006 Growing With Grammar Level 4. All Rights Reserved

Worksheet 3.5 (I or Me, We or Us) Name______________________

A. Write the pronoun **I** or **me** to complete each sentence. **(3.5)**

1. __________ will share my game with you.
2. Duncan and __________ climbed into the wagon.
3. This shirt is just right for __________.
4. That rollercoaster was too fast for Dad and __________.
5. Magda and __________ watched a film about the sun.
6. __________ need to speak with him.
7. She sat next to __________.
8. __________ was the last batter up.
9. Mom and __________ ate popcorn.
10. The gift was for Redmond and __________.

B. Write the pronoun **we** or **us** to complete each sentence. **(3.5)**

1. __________ like to babysit our cousins.
2. The dinner bell is ringing for __________.
3. __________ went to the library.
4. Ann went with Dad and __________ to the park.
5. Uncle Arnold and __________ picked strawberries.
6. __________ visited her on our way to Chicago.
7. They went to the museum with __________.
8. Grandma asked __________ for help.
9. Mom and __________ went on a picnic.
10. Karen sent a postcard to Mark and __________.

Copyright 2006 Growing With Grammar Level 4. All Rights Reserved

C. In each sentence, underline the **pronoun** and write its **antecedent** on the line. **(3.4)**

1. Martin baked his sister a cake. ______________________
2. The children flew their kites today.______________________
3. Girls, finish your lessons. ______________________
4. The dog eats its food in the laundry room.______________________
5. Mary washed her hands before eating. ______________________
6. Mrs. Lange said the puppy is hers. ______________________

D. Circle the correct **pronoun** for each sentence. **(3.1, 3.2, 3.3, 3.4, & 3.5)**

1. (She, Her) lizard ran through (our, ours) house.
2. (They, Them) found (him, his) bike.
3. Jenny and (me, I) gave the dog (it, its) bath.
4. (You, Your) directions helped Dad and (me, I).
5. (We, Us) put the luggage in (him, his) trunk.
6. (Your, Yours) fingers are cold.
7. The chickens in the pen are (ours, our).
8. Is that plate of food (mine, my)?
9. (Mine, My) aunt lives here.
10. The parakeet belongs to (hers, her).
11. (Theirs, Their) flowers are beautiful!
12. (Her, She) drew a picture of a forest.
13. The ending of the story surprised (us, we).
14. (They, Them) stayed home.

Copyright 2006 Growing With Grammar Level 4. All Rights Reserved

Worksheet 3.6 (Using Pronouns Correctly) Name____________________________

A. Circle the correct word to complete each sentence. Use the **pronoun** only when the **reference** is clear. **(3.6)**

1. Linda and Pamela raced. (She, Linda) won!
2. Barbara and Don jumped into the water. (He, Don) made a big splash.
3. Sheila helped April. (She, April) was happy.
4. Bob chased after James. (He, Bob) fell.
5. Jack and Annie made lemonade. (She, Annie) dropped the pitcher.
6. Edward and Scott read books. (He, Scott) read a mystery.
7. Stella and Mike had a garage sale. (He, Mike) sold the most.
8. Sally and Angie had a slumber party. (She, Sally) fell asleep first.
9. Kimberly and Kirk played baseball. (He, Kirk) hit a homerun.
10. Carrie and Lori play instruments. (She, Lori) plays the flute.

B. Write a **pronoun** on the line. Choose a pronoun that **clearly refers** to the noun or nouns in bold. **(3.6)**

1. The **bird** broke ____________________ wing.
2. **Janie and I** rode ____________________ scooters.
3. **I** dropped ____________________ fork on the floor.
4. **Dan** sharpened ____________________ pencil.
5. **Amber** rode ____________________ bike.
6. The **soldier** drew ____________________ sword.
7. **George** and **Martha** built a play set for ____________________ children.
8. **Tom** and **I** need to wash ____________________ clothes.
9. The **frog** stuck ____________________ tongue out.
10. **I** received a telephone call from ____________________ cousin.

Copyright 2006 Growing With Grammar Level 4. All Rights Reserved

C. Circle the correct **pronoun** for each sentence. **(3.5)**

1. (I, me) mailed the letter this morning.
2. Sandy and (I, me) took the train to Chicago.
3. Grandpa took Father and (we, us) fishing.
4. Dana told Lindsay and (I, me) about the surprise.
5. The museum tour guide and (we, us) discussed the pieces of art.
6. (We, Us) were wrong about the show time.
7. My friends and (I, me) had a disagreement.
8. Darcy waved at Elizabeth and (I, me).

D. On the line after each sentence, write the **antecedent** for the **personal pronoun** in bold. **(3.4)**

1. It is time for Albert to feed **his** parrot. ______________________
2. Gail and Adam said that **their** family has the flu. ______________________
3. I am going bowling with **my** friends. ______________________
4. Are **you** hungry, Dale? ______________________
5. Shayla is running with **her** brother. ______________________
6. The hawk spotted **its** prey. ______________________

E. Write the **plural form** of each **noun**. **(2.4, 2.5, & 2.6)**

1. tax ______________________
2. man ______________________
3. sheep ______________________
4. class ______________________
5. foot ______________________
6. noodle ______________________
7. donkey ______________________
8. watch ______________________
9. pliers ______________________
10. bunny ______________________

Copyright 2006 Growing With Grammar Level 4. All Rights Reserved

Worksheet 3.7 (Capitalization) Name__________________________

A. Rewrite these sentences using proper **capitalization**. (3.7)

1. i will be going to china in november.

____

2. uncle frank lives on breaker street.

____

3. mrs. cooley saw the empire state building in new york.

____

4. hawaii is located in the pacific ocean.

____

5. j. r. jones is my pen pal from new zealand.

____

6. aunt adelaide taught us about the planets mars and mercury.

____

7. have you ever seen mount rushmore in south dakota?

____

8. molly has an appointment today with dr. barnes.

____

Copyright 2006 Growing With Grammar Level 4. All Rights Reserved

B. Write these names correctly. **(3.7)**

1. mrs t barker ______________________
2. h r barra ______________________
3. professor flynn ______________________
4. clark a downey ______________________
5. grandma adele ______________________

C. **Diagram** the simple subjects and simple predicates in these sentences. **(1.4, 1.6, 1.7, 1.9, 1.12, & 1.14)**

1. I vacuumed and dusted the living room.
2. Did Marian leave?
3. Hang the curtains.
4. Snow and sleet fell last night.

Copyright 2006 Growing With Grammar Level 4. All Rights Reserved

Worksheet 3.8 (Capitalizing Groups, Events, and Days) Name______________________________

A. Find the **proper nouns** in these sentences and write them correctly on the line. **(3.8)**

1. The first monday in september is labor day.

____

2. I am joining the jordan soccer league this june.

____

3. We are going to the denver public library on saturday.

____

4. mom bought us a book about the revolutionary war.

____

5. Next monday we will visit the lincoln memorial.

____

6. mr. johnson flew to england for a meeting with simon's candy company.

____

7 . i watched the rose bowl parade with my uncle kenan.

____

8. We crossed the golden gate bridge when we went to san francisco.

____

9. governor roberts eats only italian food on tuesdays.

____

10. calvin lives on walnut street in new york city.

____

B. Write these words correctly using proper **capitalization**. **(3.7, & 3.8)**

1. j. m. roberts _______________________________
2. dear mrs. johnson, _______________________________
3. joe's tire company _______________________________
4. garfield junior high school _______________________________
5. american revolution _______________________________

Copyright 2006 Growing With Grammar Level 4. All Rights Reserved

C. Write a **proper noun** for each common noun. Use proper capitalization. **(3.7 & 3.8)**

1. president ______________________
2. day of the week ______________________
3. continent ______________________
4. planet ______________________
5. business/store ______________________
6. holiday ______________________
7. city ______________________
8. your initials ______________________
9. island ______________________
10. street or road ______________________

D. Write the **possessive** form of each **singular** and **plural noun**. **(2.7 & 2.8)**

1. person	______________	11. people	______________
2. man	______________	12. men	______________
3. student	______________	13. students	______________
4. mouse	______________	14. mice	______________
5. horse	______________	15. horses	______________
6. child	______________	16. children	______________
7. gorilla	______________	17. gorillas	______________
8. sister	______________	18. sisters	______________
9. aunt	______________	19. aunts	______________
10. explorer	______________	20. explorers	______________

Copyright 2006 Growing With Grammar Level 4. All Rights Reserved

Worksheet 3.9 (More Capitalization) Name____________________________

A. Underline any word that needs to be **capitalized** in each **sentence**. **(3.9)**

1. "did you see the sign on the door?" asked jessica.
2. ryan said, "i saw a crane at the cottonwood river."
3. stacy rented two movies at the henson video store.
4. we turned the wrong way on platte road.
5. i gave nicholas candy on valentine's day.
6. jani, did you eat belgian waffles at the marsden café?
7. my uncle thomas works for archer catering company.
8. aunt elizabeth leaves for italy on wednesday.
9. gerald will graduate from harvard university in may.
10. sonny's florist shop delivers flowers on mother's day.

B. Underline any word that needs to be capitalized in each **sample title** or **letter part**. **(3.9)**

1. tommy and his tall hat
2. how uncle minnow caught a fish
3. wendell the clown
4. a day at the beach
5. dear martha,
6. best regards,
7. dear mr. thomas,
8. sincerely,

C. Rewrite these words using **capital letters** where necessary. **(3.7, 3.8, & 3.9)**

1. marietta symphony ____________________
2. heinz ketchup ____________________
3. university of maine ____________________
4. memphis belle ____________________
5. milky way ____________________
6. declaration of independence ____________________
7. portugese ____________________
8. boston marathon ____________________

Copyright 2006 Growing With Grammar Level 4. All Rights Reserved

D. Below are four **topic sentences**. Write a **paragraph** about one of these sentences. Be sure to make the topic sentence that you choose the first sentence of your paragraph. Write two or three more sentences that include specific details about your topic. **(1.17)**

1. My favorite animal from Australia is ______________________.
2. A sport I would like to learn to play is______________________.
3. ______________________ is my favorite game.
4. Life as an ant would be interesting.

____

____

____

____

____

____

____

____

____

____

____

____

____

____

____

____

____

Copyright 2006 Growing With Grammar Level 4. All Rights Reserved

Worksheet 3.10 (Words That Are Not Capitalized) Name____________________

A. Underline the words in each sentence that need to be **capitalized**. (3.10)

1. marty's favorite subjects are history, spelling, and math 101.
2. bruce will take piano and the french horn lessons on the east side of town.
3. i love daisies, roses, and african violets.
4. in the winter we love to eat belgian waffles and eggs for breakfast.
5. dr. benson called to ask about my flu symptoms.
6. did mr. collins marry elizabeth in the spring?
7. i read about the mayflower at the jefferson public library in a history book.
8. jerry is a plumber at westfield plumbing store in drummond city.
9. mrs. rosemond is a judge for the city of plumfield.
10. the grocery store is south of frank's department store.
11. marcy was late for her french lesson on tuesday.
12. A spanish artist painted that mural.
13. mom made german chocolate cake for dessert.
14. darleen's mother is a professor and her father is governor hicks.

B. Rewrite these words using **capital letters** where necessary. (3.10)

1. canada goose ____________________
2. chinese checkers ____________________
3. mexican border ____________________
4. hawaiian food ____________________
5. italian dressing ____________________

Copyright 2006 Growing With Grammar Level 4. All Rights Reserved

C. Rewrite these words using **capital letters** where necessary. **(3.7, 3.8, 3.9, & 3.10)**

1. tiber river ______________________
2. american red cross ______________________
3. leaning tower of pisa ______________________
4. hoover dam ______________________
5. lincoln county hospital ______________________
6. french revolution ______________________
7. morrisville art show ______________________
8. peter j. dickinson ______________________

D. Circle the correct **pronoun** for each sentence. **(3.1, 3.2, 3.3, 3.4, & 3.5)**

1. (She, Her) bought a new book for (me, I).
2. Grandpa and (us, we) laughed at the funny joke.
3. Walter asked Ann and (I, me) a question.
4. (He, Him) searched for a spot to put up his tent.
5. Jill and (I, me) took pictures of the penguins.
6. (They, Them) sent a postcard to Mom and (us, we).

E. **Combine** each pair of sentences into a single sentence with either a **compound subject** or a **compound predicate**. **(1.8)**

1. Spoons are on the table. Napkins are on the table.

____

2. Neela watered the garden. Neela weeded the garden.

____

Copyright 2006 Growing With Grammar Level 4. All Rights Reserved

Worksheet 3.11 (Giving Directions) Name______________________________

A. Put these **directions** in order by numbering them from one to four. **(3.11)**

How to Make a Peanut Butter and Jelly Sandwich

_____ Put the slices of bread together.

_____ Spread peanut butter on one slice of bread and jelly on the other.

_____ Eat and enjoy!

_____ Get two slices of bread, peanut butter, jelly, and a butter knife.

B. Write **directions** telling how to go from your home to the grocery store. Use time order words. Be sure the directions are in the proper order and specific. **(3.11)**

____

____

____

____

____

____

____

____

____

____

____

____

____

Copyright 2006 Growing With Grammar Level 4. All Rights Reserved

C. Underline the words in each sentence that need to be **capitalized**. **(3.7, 3.8, 3.9, & 3.10)**

1. pam buys levi's jeans from noble's department store.
2. we swim every monday morning during the summer.
3. thomas has chicken pox and will miss his art class on saturday.
4. mayor thomas will speak to our group in may.
5. we need to turn west on meyer avenue to get to reese's appliance store.
6. my favorite subjects are science, spelling, english, and history.

D. Circle the **correct spelling** of the words in parentheses. Check in the **dictionary** if you are unsure. **(2.11)**

1. You need to start at the (begining, bagining, beginning).
2. Did you (remember, rememmber, remembur) your movie ticket?
3. Howard asked the actress for her (autograf, autograph, autagraph).
4. Dad bought (beautiful, buetiful, bewtiful) roses for Mom on Mother's Day.
5. (Leminade, Lemmonade, Lemonade) is my favorite drink.
6. My grandfather will (celabrate, celebrate, selebrate) his 80th birthday tomorrow.

E. **Diagram** the simple subjects and simple predicates in these sentences. **(1.4, 1.6, 1.7, 1.9, 1.12, & 1.14)**

1. Drew and Jack dusted and cleaned their room.
2. Is Karen sick?
3. Water the flowers.
4. Roses and daisies grew.

Copyright 2006 Growing With Grammar Level 4. All Rights Reserved

Chapter 3 Review Name____________________________

A. Write a **pronoun** on the lines to take the place of the repeating nouns. **(3.1)**

1. Karen ate the sandwich that Karen's mother made for Karen.

   Karen ate the sandwich that _________ mother made for_________.

2. Joe asked Joe's brother to point out the planet Saturn to Joe.

   Joe asked _________ brother to point out the planet Saturn to _________.

B. Circle the correct **pronoun** for each sentence. **(3.2)**

1. (He, Him) wrote slowly and carefully.
2. Did (them, they) eat popcorn?
3. (They, Them) love to travel.
4. Mary wrote a letter to (she, her).
5. Our cousins visit (we, us) often.
6. (It, He) is raining today.

C. Write a **pronoun** on the line to replace the noun(s) in bold in each sentence. **(3.1 & 3.2)**

1. **The children** picked strawberries. ______________________
2. **The test** was difficult. ______________________
3. **Jana** was shouting for her sister. ______________________
4. Randy ran faster than **Jim** did. ______________________
5. I bought daisies from **Mrs. Gibson**. ______________________
6. We went skating with **Dan and Kino**. ______________________

Copyright 2006 Growing With Grammar Level 4. All Rights Reserved

D. For each sentence, write a **possessive pronoun** on the line to replace the word in bold. **(3.3)**

1. This watch belongs to **me**. The watch is __________.
2. **Carrie's** bird is yellow. The yellow bird is __________.
3. The red house belongs to **us**. It is __________ house.
4. This book is __________. It is **your** book.
5. This nest belongs to the **bird**. This is __________ nest.

E. On the line after each sentence, write the **antecedent** for the **personal pronoun** in bold. **(3.4)**

1. I fell off **my** bike. ________________________
2. Matt bought **his** mouse a new cage. ________________________
3. The actress and **her** parents are nervous. ________________________
4. The bear stood on **its** hind legs. ________________________
5. The Johnsons drove **their** car many miles. ________________________

F. Write the pronoun **I** or **me** to complete each sentence. **(3.5)**

1. Will you share your cake with Bob and __________?
2. My friend and __________ went ice skating.
3. Ginny and __________ have the flu.
4. Are you studying with Peggy and __________?

G. Write the pronoun **we** or **us** to complete each sentence. **(3.5)**

1. Joe and __________ are going to Cami's birthday party.
2. The dancers and __________ practiced for two hours.
3. Everyone rushed outside to see Eli and __________.
4. The gorilla stared at Dad and __________.

Copyright 2006 Growing With Grammar Level 4. All Rights Reserved

H. Circle the correct word to complete each sentence. Use the **pronoun** only when the **reference** is clear. **(3.6)**

1. Felicia and Lana went to the zoo. (She, Lana) saw a baby elephant.
2. Juliana and Scott painted the wagon. (He, Scott) wanted to paint it blue.
3. Adam and Daniel love to jump. (He, Adam) jumps higher.
4. Justin and Missy broke the vase. (She, Missy) looked around nervously.

I. Underline any word that needs to be **capitalized** in each **sample title** or **letter part**. **(3.7)**

1. the boy in the green shirt
2. why plants drop leaves
3. the furry black kitten
4. a hot air balloon race
5. dear mark,
6. best regards,
7. dear uncle juan,
8. your friend,

J. Write these words correctly using proper **capitalization**. **(3.7, 3.8, & 3.9)**

1. rocky mountains ______________________________
2. s. g. kadar ______________________________
3. nova scotia ______________________________
4. gilbert avenue ______________________________
5. thomson high school ______________________________
6. mary's book store ______________________________
7. mayflower compact ______________________________
8. gettysburg address ______________________________
9. heinz ketchup ______________________________
10. air force one ______________________________
11. the louisville daily news ______________________________
12. labor day ______________________________

Copyright 2006 Growing With Grammar Level 4. All Rights Reserved

K. Put these **directions** in order by numbering them from one to four. **(3.11)**

How to Wash a Car

_____ Wash the car with the sponge.

_____ Dry the car with a towel.

_____ Add soap to a bucket of water.

_____ Wet a sponge with the soapy water.

Copyright 2006 Growing With Grammar Level 4. All Rights Reserved

Worksheet 4.1 (Action Verbs) Name________________________

A. Underline the **subject** once and the **verb** twice. Write **Yes** on the line if the verb is a verb you can see. Write **No** if the verb is a verb you cannot see. **(4.1)**

1. __________ The car struck the tree.
2. __________ Tony memorized the poem.
3. __________ Jerry thought of a good question.
4. __________ I learned about the Declaration of Independence today.
5. __________ Mark exercises every day.
6. __________ The children visited the museum yesterday.
7. __________ Paul forgot to finish his chores.
8. __________ The dog chased the squirrel up the tree.
9. __________ James opened the door.
10. __________ He sits at the kitchen table.

B. Write a sentence using a **verb** that shows physical action. **(4.1)**

____

____

____

____

C. Write a sentence using a **verb** that shows an action you cannot see. **(4.1)**

____

____

____

____

Copyright 2006 Growing With Grammar Level 4. All Rights Reserved

D. Underline the **action verb** in each sentence.

1. Sally called a taxicab.
2. Debra cooked an egg.
3. Janet ran to the store.
4. The seeds sprouted quickly.
5. Sam forgot his coat.
6. Kori washes the car.
7. We looked at pictures.
8. The birds sing in the morning.
9. Baily likes apple rings.
10. The people stop at the red light.
11. Lily waves at her father.
12. The kite flew over the trees.
13. Laura studies every day.
14. Betsy teaches a craft class.
15. We memorized the Declaration of Independence.
16. The goat jumped over the fence.

E. Circle the correct **pronoun** for each sentence. **(3.1 & 3.2)**

1. George said (him, he) would give (them, they) a ride to the zoo.
2. (She, Her) is the fastest runner in our neighborhood.
3. (They, Them) waited for the bus.
4. I wrote a letter to (he, him).
5. (We, Us) are going to the dance.

Copyright 2006 Growing With Grammar Level 4. All Rights Reserved

Worksheet 4.2 (Direct Objects) Name______________________________

A. In each sentence, underline the **action verb**. If there is a **direct object**, write it on the line after the sentence. **(4.2)**

1. Patrick cleaned his dirty car. ______________________________
2. Vanessa baked chocolate chip cookies. ______________________________
3. The boys played in the park. ______________________________
4. Dan ate spaghetti for dinner. ______________________________
5. Karen writes many poems. ______________________________
6. Jeremy drove carefully. ______________________________
7. Frank waved. ______________________________
8. The bird flew into the woods. ______________________________
9. We ate popcorn during the movie. ______________________________
10. The runner fell down. ______________________________
11. Bryce cleaned the windows. ______________________________
12. Kara stirred the soup. ______________________________

B. Write a **direct object** to complete each sentence. **(4.2)**

1. We saw ______________________________ at the zoo.
2. Mimi broke the ______________________________.
3. Claude stepped on the ______________________________.
4. The horses pulled the ______________________________.
5. Allan bought the ______________________________.
6. The couple built that ______________________________.
7. The dog chewed the ______________________________.
8. Kate saw a ______________________________ in the sand.

Copyright 2006 Growing With Grammar Level 4. All Rights Reserved

C. Write an **action verb** to complete each sentence. **(4.1)**

1. The airplane ______________________________at top speed.
2. Lionel ______________________________the violin in the school orchestra.
3. Jose ______________________________a beautiful song.
4. The band ______________________________onto the field.
5. The fisherman ______________________________ a shark.
6. Our neighbors ______________________________ a garden.
7. The man ______________________________ in the shade.
8. The players ______________________________ into the arena.

D. **Diagram** the subject, verb, and, if there is one, direct object in these sentences. **(1.4 & 4.2)**

1. Garrick ate hamburgers for lunch.
3. The lion roared.
2. Kristin met Arden in New York.
4. The men ran quickly.

Copyright 2006 Growing With Grammar Level 4. All Rights Reserved

Worksheet 4.3 (Linking Verbs) Name____________________________

A. Write a **linking verb** to complete each sentence. **(4.3)**

1. Callie ______________________________now a friend of mine.
2. These cookies ______________________________chocolate chip.
3. The strong wind ______________________________warm yesterday.
4. We ______________________________here last week.
5. The boys ______________________________eager to play.
6. I ______________________________terrified of spiders!
7. You ______________________________very funny.
8. She ______________________________a friendly girl.
9. Danny's favorite foods ______________________________pizza and burgers.
10. My pet ______________________________ a snail.
11. These sandwiches______________________________ peanut butter.
12. I ______________________________ a jogger.

B. Underline the **linking verb** in each sentence. **(4.3)**

1. I am the owner of a purple bicycle.
2. Mary's dog is a small poodle.
3. Those boys are my older cousins.
4. Kenji was an artist.
5. The birds were herons.
6. I am an opera singer.
7. He is an airplane pilot.
8. The white flowers are roses.

Copyright 2006 Growing With Grammar Level 4. All Rights Reserved

C. Write three sentences telling who your best friend is. Do not use verbs that show action. Underline the **linking verbs**. **(4.3)**

____

____

____

____

____

____

____

D. Underline the **verb** once. If there is a **direct object**, underline it twice. **(4.2)**

1. Elton scraped his knee.
2. My family went to the zoo.
3. The penguins jumped into the cold water.
4. The audience watched a ballet.
5. A green frog crossed the road.
6. We launched our colorful kites.

E. Underline the **topic sentence** in this **paragraph**. Cross out the sentence that really does not belong. **(1.17)**

Worker bees are very industrious insects. They feed the queen bee and keep her safe. I love to eat honey on my pancakes. They build and clean the honeycomb cells that are used for eggs. They also feed the young bees.

Copyright 2006 Growing With Grammar Level 4. All Rights Reserved

Worksheet 4.4 (Predicate Nouns) Name___________________________

A. In each sentence, underline the **linking verb**. Write the **predicate noun** on the line after the sentence. **(4.4)**

1. My sister was a dancer. ____________________
2. Those dogs are poodles. ____________________
3. Shawn is my uncle. ____________________
4. Andy is an architect. ____________________
5. That bird is a pelican. ____________________
6. My father is an artist. ____________________
7. I was a waitress. ____________________
8. Joy's mom is a firefighter. ____________________
9. These vegetables are peas. ____________________
10. Josie is my cousin. ____________________
11. My favorite dessert is chocolate ice cream. ____________________
12. Tessa is a good friend. ____________________
13. Our fort is a box. ____________________
14. The gift was a puzzle. ____________________
15. Liam is a great chef! ____________________
16. Joanne was an astronaut. ____________________

B. In each sentence, underline the **verb** once. Underline the **noun** after the verb twice. On the line after each sentence, write **DO** if the noun is a **direct object** and write **PN** if it is a **predicate noun**. **(4.2 & 4.4)**

1. My bike is a racer. __________
2. Sangita stirred the soup. __________
3. Grandpa sliced the turkey. __________
4. This building was a bank. __________
5. Lorraine visited Matilda. __________
6. Lori grabbed the rabbit. __________
7. Glyn sews clothes. __________
8. She is an engineer. __________

Copyright 2006 Growing With Grammar Level 4. All Rights Reserved

C. Underline the **verb** in each sentence. Write **Yes** if it is a verb you can see. Write **No** if it is a verb you cannot see. **(4.1)**

1. Mr. Charles worries about his garden. __________
2. The children waded in the puddle. __________
3. The firefighters entered the school. __________
4. Mary understands the question. __________
5. Harold repaired the machine. __________
6. We learned a new poem today. __________

D. **Diagram** the **subject**, **verb**, and **direct object** or **predicate noun** in each sentence. **(1.4, 4.2, & 4.4)**

1. Lorraine visited Matilda.
2. This building was a bank.
3. Joanne is my friend.
4. Lori grabbed the rabbit.

Copyright 2006 Growing With Grammar Level 4. All Rights Reserved

Worksheet 4.5 (Contractions Formed With Not) Name______________________________

A. Write **contractions** for these words. **(4.5)**

1. would not ______________________________
2. have not ______________________________
3. are not ______________________________
4. were not ______________________________
5. is not ______________________________
6. did not ______________________________
7. was not ______________________________
8. does not ______________________________
9. has not ______________________________
10. cannot ______________________________
11. do not ______________________________
12. will not ______________________________

B. Write the two words that make each **contraction**. **(4.5)**

1. shouldn't ______________________________
2. mustn't ______________________________
3. hadn't ______________________________
4. couldn't ______________________________
5. won't ______________________________
6. aren't ______________________________
7. doesn't ______________________________
8. hasn't ______________________________

Copyright 2006 Growing With Grammar Level 4. All Rights Reserved

C. Underline the **verb** in each sentence. Write **DO** if the sentence has a **direct object** or **PN** if the sentence has a **predicate noun**. **(4.2 & 4.4)**

1. Jeremy pulled the alarm. _______________
2. Aunt Allison is an art teacher. _______________
3. Mrs. Lupe's baby is a boy. _______________
4. He tells great jokes. _______________
5. Gerald is my cousin. _______________
6. The quarterback threw the ball. _______________

D. Write **directions** telling how to make a bed. Write two to four sentences telling how to do this. Use time order words like **first**, **second**, and **finally**. Make sure the directions are in the proper order. **(3.11)**

____

____

____

____

____

____

____

____

____

____

____

____

____

Copyright 2006 Growing With Grammar Level 4. All Rights Reserved

Worksheet 4.6 (Contractions Formed With Pronouns) Name________________________

A. Write the two words that make each **contraction**. **(4.6)**

1. I'm ____________________
2. you'll ____________________
3. you're ____________________
4. she's ____________________
5. it's ____________________
6. they'll ____________________
7. I'll ____________________
8. we'll ____________________
9. he's ____________________
10. you've ____________________
11. they'd ____________________
12. it'd ____________________
13. he'd ____________________
14. we've ____________________
15. they're ____________________
16. I'd ____________________
17. it'll ____________________
18. she'll ____________________
19. we're ____________________
20. we'd ____________________
21. she'd ____________________
22. he'll ____________________
23. I've ____________________
24. you'd ____________________

B. Circle the **contractions** that are written correctly. **(4.5 & 4.6)**

1. I think (shel'l, she'll) enjoy swimming in the lake.
2. You (ar'ent, aren't) supposed to open the window.
3. (We're, W'ere) going to be late for our appointment!
4. The horse (isn't, is'nt) in the barn.
5. (Theyr'e, They're) buying a new car today.
6. He (could'nt, couldn't) find his keys.
7. She (shouldn't, should'nt) eat too much chocolate.
8. (Iv'e, I've) already let the dog in.

Copyright 2006 Growing With Grammar Level 4. All Rights Reserved

C. Write three sentences telling about when you don't like to be disturbed. Use a **contraction** in each sentence. **(4.5 & 4.6)**

____

____

____

____

____

____

____

____

____

____

____

____

D. Underline the **verb** in each sentence. Write **L** if it is a **linking verb**. Write **A** if it is an **action verb**. **(4.1 & 4.3)**

1. Priya is a great singer. ____________
2. We walked ten miles. ____________
3. The boys made a sand castle. ____________
4. Alayna wrote an essay. ____________
5. The clothes are dry. ____________
6. Jane was my best friend. ____________

Copyright 2006 Growing With Grammar Level 4. All Rights Reserved

Worksheet 4.7 (Helping Verbs) Name________________________

A. Underline the **main verbs** once and the **helping verbs** twice. **(4.7)**

1. Carmen will jog for twenty minutes today.
2. I have left my jacket at home.
3. You should have watched that movie with us.
4. Terry must have finished his lessons early.
5. The squirrel has eaten the nut.
6. Jamie will be going to the baseball game.
7. Sally can mow the lawn now.
8. The boys were waiting at the bus stop.

B. Circle the correct **helping verb** for each sentence. **(4.7)**

1. I (am, will) clean my room today.
2. Willa (had, were) gotten up before the alarm went off.
3. He (has, is) worked at the grocery store for two weeks.
4. We (did, have) been reading about pirates.
5. Adrian (am, will) have run three miles by the end of the day.
6. Stella (has, might) been taking gymnastics for five years.
7. The cats (would, were) sleeping on the porch.
8. The players (are, am) talking to the coach.

C. Write two sentences using two of these **helping verbs**: **is are was were have did**

1. ____

____

2. ____

____

Copyright 2006 Growing With Grammar Level 4. All Rights Reserved

D. Write as many of the 23 **helping verbs** as you can remember. The first letter of each word has been provided. A few of the helping verbs have been completed for you. **(4.7)**

a m	h __ __ __	d __	s __ __ __ __	m __ __
i __	h a s	d __ __ __	w i l l	m __ __ __ __
a __ __	h __ __	d __ __	s __ __ __ __ __	m __ __ __
w __ __			w __ __ __ __	c a n
w __ __ __				c __ __ __ __
b __				
b __ __ __ __				
b __ __ __				

E. Write **contractions** for these words. **(4.5 & 4.6)**

1. he will ____________________
2. I am ____________________
3. do not ____________________
4. you are ____________________
5. it would ____________________
6. would not ____________________
7. will not ____________________
8. we are ____________________

F. **Diagram** the **subject**, **verb**, and **direct object** or **predicate noun** in each sentence. **(1.4, 4.2, & 4.4)**

1. My uncle is a teacher.
2. Fernando caught five fish.
3. I bought a new skateboard.
4. This flower is a daisy.

Copyright 2006 Growing With Grammar Level 4. All Rights Reserved

Worksheet 4.8 (Verb Phrases) Name______________________

A. Underline the **verb phrase** for each sentence. Write the **helping verbs** on the line. **(4.8)**

1. David was not listening to his radio. ______________________
2. Shawn has been staying with his grandparents. ______________________
3. The money was not stolen from the bank. ______________________
4. Evan might eat at our house. ______________________
5. The airplane should be landing soon. ______________________
6. The baby hasn't been crying all night. ______________________
7. My watch was found under the couch. ______________________
8. Lane isn't leaving on vacation tomorrow. ______________________
9. The wagon had not been painted red. ______________________
10. Her leg might have been broken when she fell. ______________________
11. Jane will be staying overnight. ______________________
12. We have not been playing with those toys. ______________________
13. She must have been cleaning all day. ______________________
14. I could not complete my math test. ______________________
15. You should have been mowing the lawn. ______________________
16. We can make ice cream sundaes. ______________________
17. You should not sit in that chair. ______________________
18. Sheryl has been sweeping the porch. ______________________
19. Doug should not have called his mother. ______________________
20. Joy will be using the watercolors. ______________________

Copyright 2006 Growing With Grammar Level 4. All Rights Reserved

B. Write a **helping verb** on the line for each **action verb** in bold. **(4.7 & 4.8)**

1. She ______________ **learning** about the water cycle.
2. The clowns ______________ **entertaining** the crowd.
3. I ______________ **going** to a cookout.
4. Jared ______________ **eaten** the entire pie.
5. The pencil ______________ **broken** by him.
6. They ______________ **repairing** the fence.
7. George ______________ **visited** his friend in Italy.
8. We ______________ **touring** the candy factory today.

C. Write **contractions** for these words. **(4.5 & 4.6)**

1. I am ______________	7. has not ______________
2. you will ______________	8. must not ______________
3. she would ______________	9. they have ______________
4. will not ______________	10. does not ______________
5. we are ______________	11. it has ______________
6. he is ______________	12. cannot ______________

D. Rewrite these **quotations**. Be sure to add capital letters, commas, quotation marks, and end punctuation. **(1.15)**

1. i have never seen Lake Ontario said John

____

2. is Janie at the beach asked Carl

____

3. mariah exclaimed i lost my ring

____

Copyright 2006 Growing With Grammar Level 4. All Rights Reserved

Worksheet 4.9 (Verb Tenses) Name_______________________

A. For each sentence, write **Past**, **Present**, or **Future** to show the **tense** of the **verb** in bold. **(4.9)**

1. We **lived** in Illinois for two years. _______________
2. Dad **will fix** my bike tomorrow. _______________
3. The children **hurried** to finish their chores. _______________
4. Brandon **eats** quickly. _______________
5. They **decided** to leave early. _______________
6. I **shall fly** my kite. _______________
7. Mom **called** us in for dinner. _______________
8. The boys **climb** up the rope. _______________
9. Tony **throws** the ball. _______________
10. My sisters **raced** across the field. _______________
11. He **parked** the car. _______________
12. Lydia **will paint** a picture. _______________
13. I **collect** stamps. _______________
14. Bob **makes** model ships. _______________

B. Write the **past tense** form of these verbs. **(4.9)**

1. try _______________
2. jump _______________
3. wash _______________
4. camp _______________
5. study _______________
6. stop _______________
7. hurry _______________
8. wrap _______________

C. Read each sentence. Write on the line whether the **progressive verb form** in bold is **present**, **past**, or **future**.

1. It **was raining** when we left home. _______________
2. I **will be eating** dinner soon. _______________
3. Shelby **is sitting** on the couch. _______________
4. You **are talking** quickly. _______________

Copyright 2006 Growing With Grammar Level 4. All Rights Reserved

D. Write three sentences using **verbs** in the **past tense** to tell about a sporting event you have seen or played in recently. **(4.9)**

____

____

____

____

____

____

____

____

____

E. Write an **X** next to the **helping verbs**. **(4.7)**

1. _____ being	5. _____ shall	9. _____ stop	13. _____ had
2. _____ can	6. _____ wait	10. _____ am	14. _____ fly
3. _____ is	7. _____ have	11. _____ fall	15. _____ be
4. _____ run	8. _____ was	12. _____ do	16. _____ will

F. Rewrite these sentences to show **future tense**. **(4.9)**

1. George leaves for college tomorrow.

____

2. I make peanut butter cookies.

____

Copyright 2006 Growing With Grammar Level 4. All Rights Reserved

Worksheet 4.10 (Irregular Verbs) Name____________________________

A. Circle the correct **past tense** of the **irregular verbs** in these sentences. **(4.10)**

1. The flowers (growed, grew) quickly.
2. We (leaved, left) the library at noon.
3. Jerry (knowed, knew) the answer to the question.
4. The boys (hid, hided) in the pantry.
5. Kara (sent, sended) a letter to her friend in Nebraska.
6. Joey (goed, went) down the slide with his brother.
7. The spider (built, builded) an amazing web.
8. I (comed, came) home as fast as I could.
9. Mom (telled, told) me how to make a salad.
10. The dog (bit, bited) the mailman's shoe.
11. We (catched, caught) a scorpion in the house!
12. Carmine has (broke, breaked) his baseball bat.
13. I (rided, rode) that rollercoaster five times.
14. Our team (winned, won) the game!

B. Write the **past tense** form of these **verbs**. **(4.9 & 4.10)**

1. teach ____________________	6. end ____________________
2. hold ____________________	7. try ____________________
3. laugh ____________________	8. slip ____________________
4. pay ____________________	9. see ____________________
5. say ____________________	10. cry ____________________

Copyright 2006 Growing With Grammar Level 4. All Rights Reserved

C. Below are four **topic sentences**. Write a **paragraph** about one of these sentences. Be sure to make the topic sentence you choose the first sentence of your paragraph. Write two or three more sentences that include specific details about your topic. **(1.17)**

1. Something fun I enjoy doing with my family is ________________________.
2. If I had a time machine I would ________________________.
3. ______________________ is my favorite book.
4. My favorite family dinner is_____________________.

____

____

____

____

____

____

____

____

____

____

____

____

____

____

____

____

____

____

____

Copyright 2006 Growing With Grammar Level 4. All Rights Reserved

Worksheet 4.11 (Using Irregular Verbs) Name____________________________

A. Write the correct **past tense** for the **verb** in parentheses. **(4.11)**

1. The worm has (eat) a hole in the leaf. ____________________
2. I have (see) that movie already. ____________________
3. Shane has (break) his arm. ____________________
4. We have (sing) this song before. ____________________
5. The tomato plants have (grow) large. ____________________
6. She has (ride) her bike to the pool all week. ____________________
7. John has (catch) a cold from his sister. ____________________
8. We had (bring) too much food to the picnic. ____________________
9. I (teach) my sister how to tie her shoes today. ____________________
10. Ronan has (make) his bed already. ____________________
11. The girls (draw) pictures of each other. ____________________
12. Jeff has (throw) the baseball. ____________________

B. Write the **past tense** form of these **verbs**. **(4.10 & 4.11)**

1. stand ____________________________
2. buy ____________________________
3. spend ____________________________
4. keep ____________________________
5. fight ____________________________
6. make ____________________________
7. lose ____________________________
8. hold ____________________________

Copyright 2006 Growing With Grammar Level 4. All Rights Reserved

C. Write three sentences about a birthday party you have attended. Use different forms of the verbs **go**, **sing**, and **eat**. **(4.11)**

____

____

____

____

____

____

____

____

____

D. Write an X next to the **helping verbs**. **(4.7)**

1. _____ has	5. _____ was	9. _____ these	13. _____ not
2. _____ does	6. _____ been	10. _____ those	14. _____ can
3. _____ bad	7. _____ that	11. _____ shall	15. _____ will
4. _____ many	8. _____ should	12. _____ this	16. _____ might

E. Underline the **verb phrase** in each sentence. **(4.8)**

1. Kim has invited us to her birthday party.
2. Mrs. Morgan will not be helping us with our garage sale.
3. Caleb is studying three languages.
4. We should be finishing our lunch.
5. I have not sorted the laundry.
6. Dad is growing corn in our garden.

Copyright 2006 Growing With Grammar Level 4. All Rights Reserved

Worksheet 4.12 (Subject – Verb Agreement) Name________________________

A. Circle the correct **verb** for each sentence. **(4.12)**

1. This food (taste, tastes) great!
2. He (run, runs) the local grocery store.
3. The baseball players (work, works) well together.
4. The frog (wait, waits) patiently for its food.
5. Kamaria and Shani (walk, walks) to the library together.
6. She (take, takes) her sister to practice on Tuesdays.
7. Three birds (live, lives) in the birdhouse I made.
8. My family (travel, travels) to Europe every year.
9. The dog (search, searches) for its bone.
10. Valerie (practice, practices) the violin every day.
11. They (make, makes) fudge for the bake sale.
12. The nurses (examine, examines) the patient.

B. Write the correct form of the **verb** in parentheses. **(4.12)**

1. Camels (live) in Africa. ________________________
2. Grandpa (fish) every day. ________________________
3. Jasper (use) his computer for his lessons. ________________________
4. Courtney and Emma (swim) on a team. ________________________
5. The explorer (dig) for gold. ________________________
6. We (collect) shells when we are at the beach. ________________________
7. Mary (sing) in a band. ________________________
8. I (like) scrambled eggs and toast. ________________________

Copyright 2006 Growing With Grammar Level 4. All Rights Reserved

C. For each sentence, write **Past**, **Present**, or **Future** to show the **tense** of the **verb** in bold. **(4.9)**

1. The dog **licks** my hand. ______________________
2. He **will open** the jelly jar. ______________________
3. Dorian **closed** the window. ______________________
4. I **shall try** my best. ______________________
5. The boys **ride** their bikes. ______________________

D. Underline the **verb** in each sentence. Write **L** if it is a **linking verb**. Write **A** if it is an **action verb**. **(4.1 & 4.3)**

1. Evan is my brother. ____________
2. Mr. Donnellson was a salesperson. ____________
3. Clio built a sandcastle. ____________
4. Melanie is our leader. ____________
5. The king enters his palace. ____________
6. A snake hissed at me. ____________

E. **Diagram** the **subject**, **verb**, and **direct object** or **predicate noun** in each sentence. **(1.4, 4.2, & 4.4)**

1. Evan is my brother.
3. Melanie is our leader.
2. Clio built a sandcastle.
4. The king enters his palace.

Copyright 2006 Growing With Grammar Level 4. All Rights Reserved

Worksheet 4.13 (The Verb Have) Name__________________________

A. Circle the correct form of the verb **have** for each sentence. **(4.13)**

1. The children (had, has) a great time!
2. I think we (has, have) enough money.
3. The bee (have, has) stung Donna.
4. Do you (have, has) a headache?
5. Thomas (have, had) taken a shower already.
6. Timmy (have, has) written a letter to his friend.
7. The bird (has, have) a broken wing.
8. Our plane (has, have) landed on time.
9. The boys (had, has) tennis lessons this afternoon.
10. Brenna (have, has) brown hair.

B. Write <u>**H**</u> if the verb in bold is a **helping verb**. Write <u>**M**</u> if it is the **main verb**. **(4.13)**

1. _____ Charlie **has** changed his shoes.
2. _____ The children **have** played all afternoon.
3. _____ My family **has** driven across the United States.
4. _____ Mary **had** a snack.
5. _____ We **have** completed the project.
6. _____ Pat **has** cleaned his car.
7. _____ She **had** sent a card to her cousin.
8. _____ Gemma **has** a cold.
9. _____ I **have** a great idea!
10. _____ Janine **has** acted in a commercial.

Copyright 2006 Growing With Grammar Level 4. All Rights Reserved

C. Write two sentences. Use **has** as a **main verb** in the first sentence and as a **helping verb** in the second sentence. **(4.13)**

____

____

____

____

D. Circle the correct **verb** for each sentence. **(4.12)**

1. The fans (cheer, cheers) for the football team.
2. He (deliver, delivers) newspapers on the weekends.
3. I (wear, wears) a helmet when I (ride, rides) my bike.
4. The boys (splash, splashes) in the pool.
5. My family (eat, eats) dinner together every night.
6. Jenny (smile, smiles) at everyone she meets.
7. Herbert (need, needs) new eye glasses.
8. The movies (begin, begins) in thirty minutes.
9. Dad (drive, drives) us to the beach in the summer.
10. We (make, makes) lemonade when we are thirsty.

E. In each sentence, underline the **action verb**. If there is a **direct object**, write it on the line after the sentence. **(4.2)**

1. Pedro walks every day. ____________________
2. The frog caught a fly. ____________________
3. A deer raised its head. ____________________
4. The cows grazed in the meadow. ____________________
5. Our neighbors sold their house. ____________________
6. The band marched quickly. ____________________

Copyright 2006 Growing With Grammar Level 4. All Rights Reserved

Worksheet 4.14 (The Verb Do) Name___________________________

A. Circle the correct form of the verb **do** for each sentence. **(4.14)**

1. Benjamin (do, does) his job well.
2. My friend (do, does) live on a farm.
3. The crowds (does, did) wait for hours.
4. (Do, Does) you want to listen to the orchestra?
5. She (do, did) the dishes.
6. We (does, did) study about the water cycle.
7. I always (does, do) what I am told.
8. We (did, does) eat cheeseburgers.
9. (Did, Does) you brush your teeth?
10. Maia (do, does) cartwheels.

B. Write H if the verb in bold is a **helping verb**. Write M if it is the **main verb**. **(4.14)**

1. _____ I **do** the shopping for my family.
2. _____ Troy **did** his own laundry.
3. _____ Marianne **does** need a new hairbrush.
4. _____ You **did** that perfectly!
5. _____ They **did** walk to the pond.
6. _____ She **does** her best.
7. _____ I **do** ride the bus on Saturday.
8. _____ Boris **did** drive to a friend's house.
9. _____ The girls **did** swim today.
10. _____ Donald **does** the vacuuming.

Copyright 2006 Growing With Grammar Level 4. All Rights Reserved

C. Write the **verb phrase** for each sentence on the line. **(4.8)**

1. The sharks were swimming in shallow water. ______________________
2. The girls are not cleaning their mess. ______________________
3. We have been watching a ballet. ______________________
4. A pilot is flying the airplane. ______________________
5. You shouldn't have stepped in the puddle. ______________________
6. This might not cost too much. ______________________
7. The skiers were climbing the hill. ______________________
8. A bear had been sleeping in the cave. ______________________

D. **Diagram** the **subject**, **verb**, and **direct object** or **predicate noun** in each sentence.
(1.4, 1.12, 4.2, & 4.4)

1. The skiers were climbing the hill.
2. She did the dishes.
3. This room was the kitchen.
4. Charlie has changed his shoes.
5. Mom is my teacher.
6. Did you brush your teeth?

Copyright 2006 Growing With Grammar Level 4. All Rights Reserved

Worksheet 4.15 (Writing a Narrative Paragraph) Name_______________________

A. Below are three **topic sentences**. Write a **narrative paragraph** about one of these sentences. Be sure to make the topic sentence you choose the first sentence of your paragraph. Write two or three more sentences that help to tell a story about your topic. **(4.15)**

1. The first time I rode a bicycle_______________________.
2. This is how_______________________ and I became friends.
3. My most serious accident happened when_______________________.

____

____

____

____

____

____

____

____

____

____

____

____

____

____

____

____

____

____

____

Copyright 2006 Growing With Grammar Level 4. All Rights Reserved

B. Circle the correct **present tense verb** for each sentence. **(4.9)**

1. Nathaniel (lift, lifts) the garage door.
2. My brothers (laugh, laughs) at my jokes.
3. Dad (watch, watches) the evening news every night.
4. Enrique (play, plays) golf at noon.
5. We (plant, plants) flowers in the front yard

C. Write the two words that make each **contraction**. **(4.5 & 4.6)**

1. hadn't ____________________
2. isn't ____________________
3. you're ____________________
4. they're ____________________
5. weren't ____________________
6. don't ____________________
7. I'll ____________________
8. you'll ____________________
9. haven't ____________________
10. couldn't ____________________
11. didn't ____________________
12. he's ____________________

D. Add **quotation marks** to these sentences. Underline the **speaker tags**. **(1.15)**

1. Have you fed your pet rabbit? asked Landon.
2. Jasper said, Help me take out the trash.
3. Don't forget your umbrella, said Mom.
4. Kathleen exclaimed, The stove is hot!
5. Tina asked, Are those coins rare?
6. Has Warren done the dishes? asked Dad.

Copyright 2006 Growing With Grammar Level 4. All Rights Reserved

Chapter 4 Review

Name____________________________

A. Underline the **subject** once and the **verb** twice. Write **Yes** on the line if the verb is a verb you can see. Write **No** if the verb is a verb you cannot see. **(4.1)**

1. __________ Avery memorized a poem.
2. __________ We learned about knights.
3. __________ Marty writes letters.
4. __________ Jemma eats grapes.
5. __________ I know the answer.
6. __________ Dad makes ice cream.

B. In each sentence, underline the **action verb**. If there is a **direct object**, write it on the line after the sentence. **(4.1 & 4.2)**

1. Satchel filled the stapler. ____________________
2. The children rushed outside. ____________________
3. The cat ran across the street. ____________________
4. Camika broke the chair. ____________________
5. The plumber fixed the sink. ____________________

C. Write a **linking verb** to complete each sentence. **(4.3)**

1. We ________________________ right behind him yesterday.
2. My aunt ________________________ a tour guide at the museum.
3. Some snakes ________________________ venomous.
4. Hawaii ________________________ our favorite vacation destination.
5. Elijah ________________________ sorry about the accident.

D. In each sentence, underline the **linking verb**. Write the **predicate noun** on the line after the sentence **(4.3 & 4.4)**

1. He is a clever boy. ____________________
2. Marjorie is a great chef. ____________________
3. The meat is chicken. ____________________
4. Sally was the winner. ____________________
5. My cousin is a teacher. ____________________

Copyright 2006 Growing With Grammar Level 4. All Rights Reserved

E. Write the two words that make each **contraction**. **(4.5 & 4.6)**

1. won't ____________________ 6. couldn't ____________________
2. you're ____________________ 7. I'm ____________________
3. he's ____________________ 8. wasn't ____________________
4. can't ____________________ 9. we've ____________________
5. he'd ____________________ 10. they'd ____________________

F. Underline the main **verbs** once and the **helping verbs** twice. **(4.7)**

1. We have decorated the parade float with flowers.
2. The race had ended in a flash.
3. Jonah was smiling from ear to ear.
4. Moira will be helping us.
5. You should have been playing tag with the boys.

G. Write the **verb phrase** for each sentence on the line. **(4.8)**

1. Stacy was not worried about the mess. ________________________
2. Karl isn't helping us. ________________________
3. The musicians have not learned the music. ________________________
4. The butterfly hasn't landed. ________________________
5. We weren't waiting for Timothy. ________________________

H. For each sentence, write **Past**, **Present**, or **Future** to show the **tense** of the **verb** in bold. **(4.9)**

1. Jamie **jogged** for two hours. ____________________
2. They **will make** brownies for dessert. ____________________
3. We **hiked** into the forest. ____________________
4. Audrey **talks** very fast. ____________________
5. You **will find** your coat in the closet. ____________________

Copyright 2006 Growing With Grammar Level 4. All Rights Reserved

I. Read each sentence. Write on the line whether the **progressive verb form** in bold is **present**, **past**, or **future**.

1. We **were baking** cookies. ____________________
2. She **was dancing** when the doorbell rang. ____________________
3. Henry **is reading** his favorite book. ____________________
4. Dad **will be eating** soon. ____________________

J. Circle the correct **past tense** of the **irregular verbs** in these sentences. **(4.10 & 4.11)**

1. I was (bited, bitten) by a mosquito.
2. Troy (spent, spended) his birthday money on a bicycle.
3. Dad's car has (broked, broken) down.
4. We (built, builted) a tree house in the backyard.
5. Diego (taught, teached) me how to ride a skateboard.
6. Sandra (won, winned) the spelling bee.

K. Circle the correct **verb** for each sentence. **(4.12)**

1. She (serve, serves) fresh bread.
2. Trees (sway, sways) in the wind.
3. People (jog, jogs) down the street.
4. He (empty, empties) the trash.
5. The bird (stay, stays) in its cage.
6. The athletes (run, runs) on the track.

L. Write H if the verb in bold is a **helping verb**. Write M if it is the **main verb**. **(4.13 & 4.14)**

1. ______ I **have** a toothache.
2. ______ Aaron **did** his chores after dinner.
3. ______ She **does** run fast!
4. ______ Marie **has** watered the plants.
5. ______ Morgan **has** brushed her hair.
6. ______ My dog **has** fleas.
7. ______ **Did** you finish the dishes?
8. ______ **Have** you fed the cat?

Copyright 2006 Growing With Grammar Level 4. All Rights Reserved

M. **Diagram** the **subject**, **verb**, and **direct object** or **predicate noun** in each sentence. **(1.4, 1.12, 4.2, & 4.4)**

1. My cousin is a teacher.

2. Have you fed the cat?

3. Camika broke the chair.

4. Audrey talks very fast.

Copyright 2006 Growing With Grammar Level 4. All Rights Reserved

Worksheet 5.1 (Adjectives) Name________________________

A. Write **Whose**, **Which One**, **How Many**, or **What Kind** to tell what type of adjective is in bold. **(5.1)**

1. **White** pebbles were on the road. ________________
2. **Four** cows roamed in the field. ________________
3. We live in the **third** house. ________________
4. Put **these** vases on the shelf. ________________
5. **Some** children rang the doorbell and ran. ________________
6. **My** sister lost a tooth. ________________
7. Jeremy stubbed **his** toe. ________________
8. We went into a **dark** cave. ________________
9. **This** road is closed. ________________
10. The **first** day of the month is my birthday. ________________
11. **Several** people came to the play. ________________
12. **Her** team won the tournament. ________________
13. We are going to **that** restaurant. ________________
14. **Matt's** dog barked all night. ________________

B. Circle the correct **articles** to complete these sentences. **(5.1)**

1. Joe has (a, an) pet bird and (a, an) iguana.
2. (The, An) movie about (a, an) alligator is on in five minutes.
3. Dylan won (a, an) trophy in (a, the) art contest.
4. (An, The) baseball player hit (a, an) homerun.
5. (An, A) elephant ran from (a, an) small mouse.
6. Do you want (the, an) grapes or (a, an) apple?

Copyright 2006 Growing With Grammar Level 4. All Rights Reserved

C. Circle the correct **order of adjectives** in the following sentences. **(5.1)**

1. Tony is a (tall thin) (thin tall) man.
2. The boys love eating (red large) (large red) raspberries.
3. Shelby's dog is a (small tan Austrian) (Austrian small tan) hound.
4. We climbed the (large green) (green large) tree.

D. Underline the **adjectives** in each sentence. **(5.1)**

1. Two birds were in this tall tree.
2. We drank cold lemonade and ate spicy food.
3. That red ball bounced across our road.
4. Bailey's parents bought some yellow fish.
5. We will live in that new home in three months.

E. **Combine** or rewrite these sentences into one grammatically correct sentence that is either a) a **compound sentence** or b) includes either a **compound subject**, or **compound predicate**. **(1.8 & 1.10)**

1. Bob was not tall he was a great basketball player.

____

2. Ash blew into the sky. Lava blew into the sky.

____

3. The boy picked the tomato. The boy ate the tomato.

____

Copyright 2006 Growing With Grammar Level 4. All Rights Reserved

Worksheet 5.2 (Diagramming Adjectives) Name___________________________

A. Diagram these sentences. **(1.4, 1.6, 1.12, 4.2, 4.4, & 5.2)**

1. The young boy carried three pictures.
2. Susan and Julie are best friends.
3. The girls are eating two sweet oranges.
4. Bailey's parents bought some yellow fish.
5. Gerald was a great instructor.
6. My big sister picked a fragrant rose.
7. Did you take my blue pen?
8. My sister lost a tooth.

Copyright 2006 Growing With Grammar Level 4. All Rights Reserved

B. Underline the **adjectives** in each sentence. **(5.1)**

1. The new car has red paint.
2. My brown dog is chasing that yellow cat.
3. Several people caught large white fish.
4. Your little brother broke my three red pencils.
5. The second girl is my favorite cousin.
6. Ten brown beavers chew crunchy bark.
7. White fluffy clouds floated overhead.
8. Cold lemonade and bologna sandwiches were served.
9. Five red fish swam in my new aquarium.
10. Hungry birds searched for juicy worms.
11. Jo's brown bunny hopped into its large cage.
12. The sick child slept on this couch.
13. I am the third child in my large family.
14. Do we have enough flour to make some cookies?
15. The tall girl in the blue car stopped at the red light.
16. The last game was played on a cold day.

C. Write the correct **article <u>a</u>** or **<u>an</u>** before each word. **(5.1)**

1. ______________ picture
2. ______________ lamp
3. ______________ envelope
4. ______________ astronaut
5. ______________ rabbit
6. ______________ job
7. ______________ index
8. ______________ artist
9. ______________ igloo
10. ______________ umbrella
11. ______________ book
12. ______________ egg
13. ______________ alligator
14. ______________ day
15. ______________ word
16. ______________ author

Copyright 2006 Growing With Grammar Level 4. All Rights Reserved

Worksheet 5.3 (This, That, These, and Those) Name____________________________

A. Circle the correct word for each sentence. **(5.3)**

1. (This, Those) story tells about a lost boy.
2. (Those, That) flower smells wonderful!
3. Are (these, this) your earrings?
4. Does (this, these) shirt still fit you?
5. (That, These) store sells delicious candy.
6. (That, These) quarters are part of my collection.
7. (This, Those) puppies need to be fed.
8. (This, Those) postcard is for you.
9. (That, Those) chair belongs in the living room.
10. (These, This) tree is fun to climb on.
11. (These, This) towels are for the beach.
12. (That, Those) eggs were delicious.

B. Cross out the word that does not belong in each sentence. **(5.3)**

1. Is that there a woodpecker?
2. This here is a friendly dog.
3. Those there birds are ostriches.
4. These here books are mine.
5. I like this here car.
6. That there toast is delicious.
7. These here tools are Dad's.
8. Those there snacks are for sale.

Copyright 2006 Growing With Grammar Level 4. All Rights Reserved

C. Write four sentences that describe your bedroom. Use the adjectives **this**, **that**, **these**, and **those** in your sentences. **(5.3)**

____

____

____

____

____

____

____

____

D. Diagram these sentences. **(1.4, 1.6, 1.12, 4.2, 4.4, & 5.2)**

1. Squirrels and chipmunks eat brown nuts.
2. My brothers are eating this chocolate pie.
3. That happy clown made a funny face.
4. Did that girl wear a red dress?
5. Some birds ate two juicy worms.
6. Regina is a beautiful ballerina.

Copyright 2006 Growing With Grammar Level 4. All Rights Reserved

Worksheet 5.4 (Proper Adjectives) Name________________________

A. Underline the **proper adjective** in each sentence. Write the **noun** it describes on the line. **(5.4)**

1. Mom's Thanksgiving turkey tastes delicious. ____________________
2. My aunt lives near the Mexican border. ____________________
3. Greek pastry is Joe's favorite dessert. ____________________
4. Mary saw the Roman ruins on her vacation. ____________________
5. Maria's mom makes great Italian food. ____________________
6. The Asian continent is the largest in the world. ____________________
7. Are you wearing a Scottish kilt? ____________________
8. Grandma made Belgian waffles for breakfast. ____________________
9. Mrs. Marsh raises African violets. ____________________
10. We had dinner in an Indian restaurant. ____________________

B. Change these proper nouns into **proper adjectives**. Check the dictionary if you are unsure of the spelling. **(5.4)**

1. Japan ________________________________
2. Sweden ________________________________
3. Canada ________________________________
4. Asia ________________________________
5. China ________________________________
6. Turkey ________________________________
7. England ________________________________
8. Australia ________________________________
9. France ________________________________
10. America ________________________________

Copyright 2006 Growing With Grammar Level 4. All Rights Reserved

C. Write **this** or **these** to tell about nouns that express nearness. **(5.3)**

1. ______________________ spider is poisonous.
2. I think ______________________ flowers are for you.
3. The rabbit is hiding behind ______________________ bushes.
4. Did you read ______________________ story about a pioneer family?

D. Write **that** or **those** to tell about nouns that express distance. **(5.3)**

1. What is the title of ______________________ poem?
2. ______________________ strawberries are enormous!
3. How did ______________________ fly get in the house?
4. I think ______________________ crayons belong to Evan.

E. Underline the **verb** in each sentence. Write **DO** if the sentence has a **direct object** or **PN** if the sentence has a **predicate noun**. **(4.2 & 4.4)**

1. These books are mystery novels. ______________
2. My uncle is a teacher. ______________
3. I bought a new skateboard. ______________
4. This flower is a daisy. ______________
5. Fernando caught five fish. ______________
6. Jeremy pulled the alarm. ______________
7. Mrs. Lupe's baby is a boy. ______________
8. He tells great jokes. ______________
9. Gerald is my cousin. ______________
10. The quarterback threw the ball. ______________

Copyright 2006 Growing With Grammar Level 4. All Rights Reserved

Worksheet 5.5 (Adjectives that Compare) Name______________________________

A. Circle the correct form of the **adjective** for each sentence. **(5.5)**

1. Today is the (hotter, hottest, most hottest) day of the week.
2. Jeremy is the (faster, fastest, most fastest) boy I know.
3. My Mom is the (nicer, nicest, most nicest) person in the world!
4. Julian is (helpfuller, more helpful, most helpful) than Aaron.
5. Dad is (more older, older, oldest) than Uncle Jeff.
6. That was the (easier, easiest, most easiest) test I have ever taken.
7. I am (more careful, carefuller, most careful) now than I used to be.
8. Shawna has the (most beautiful, beautifulest) singing voice we have ever heard.
9. Jerome is (more taller, taller, tallest) than Cooper.
10. These cookies are (deliciouser, more delicious, most delicious) than those cookies.
11. George is the (most odd, odder, oddest) man I have ever met.
12. Jason is (excited, more excited, most excited) about the carnival than Joe.
13. Your bathing suit is (more wetter, wetter, wettest) than mine.
14. This bear is (more friendlier, friendlier, friendliest) than that one.
15. The (most smartest, smarter, smartest) boy of all is Ryan.
16. The roads are (icier, iciest, more icier) today than they were yesterday.
17. A watermelon is (more bigger, bigger, biggest) than a strawberry.
18. That is the (stranger, strangest, most strangest) animal I have ever seen.
19. Anthony is the (greater, greatest, most greatest) friend I have.
20. This play is (more enjoyable, most enjoyable, enjoyabler) than the last one.

Copyright 2006 Growing With Grammar Level 4. All Rights Reserved

B. Write three sentences that compare a snake to a worm. Use **adjectives** to compare them. **(5.5)**

C. Write the two words that make each **contraction**. **(4.5 & 4.6)**

1. weren't
2. they've

R 3. we're

4. wouldn't
5. didn't
6. he'll
7. it's
8. you're
9. won't
10. doesn't

Copyright 2006 Growing With Grammar Level 4. All Rights Reserved

Worksheet 5.6 (Forming Adjectives that Compare) Name_______________________

A. Write the comparative and superlative forms of these **adjectives**. **(5.6)**

Examples: mean → meaner meanest
patient → more patient most patient

1. big _______________ _______________
2. funny _______________ _______________
3. happy _______________ _______________
4. rough _______________ _______________
5. short _______________ _______________
6. popular _______________ _______________
7. beautiful _______________ _______________
8. intelligent _______________ _______________
9. warm _______________ _______________
10. serious _______________ _______________
11. large _______________ _______________
12. exciting _______________ _______________
13. cheerful _______________ _______________
14. good _______________ _______________
15. bad _______________ _______________
16. many _______________ _______________
17. much _______________ _______________
18. little _______________ _______________

B. Complete each sentence with **more** or **most**. **(5.6)**

1. Ben is _______________ mysterious than Mattie.
2. That is the _______________ colorful bird I have ever seen.
3. Linda and Pam are the _______________ talkative girls on my street.
4. This puppy is _______________ playful than that one.
5. The whale shark is the _______________ gigantic fish of all.

Copyright 2006 Growing With Grammar Level 4. All Rights Reserved

C. Circle the correct form of the **adjective** for each sentence. **(5.5 & 5.6)**

1. Joe is a (good, better, best) catcher than Elliot.
2. You are the (better, bestest, best) friend Josie has.
3. He has the (much, more, most) lemonade of all.
4. What city has the (worse, worst, worstest) weather?
5. Armand has (more, morer, most) freckles than his sister.
6. That is the (good, better, best) restaurant in town.
7. He has the (less, least, leastest) amount of ice cream.
8. This is the (good, better, best) play I have ever seen.
9. This parakeet makes (little, less, least) noise than that parakeet.
10. Veronica is having the (much, more, most) fun ever.

D. **Diagram** these sentences. **(1.4, 4.4, & 5.2)**

1. That animal is a dog.

3. That is a dog.

2. Those flowers are roses.

4. Those are roses.

Copyright 2006 Growing With Grammar Level 4. All Rights Reserved

Worksheet 5.7 (Adjective Suffixes) Name________________________

A. Add the **suffix -able**, **-ful**, or **-less** to the underlined base word to find the correct word for each definition. **(5.7)**

Example: full of joy → joyful

1. without speech ________________________
2. able to comfort ________________________
3. full of success ________________________
4. without help ________________________
5. can drink ________________________
6. full of cheer ________________________
7. without point ________________________
8. able to depend ________________________
9. can wash ________________________
10. without fear ________________________

B. Circle the correct meaning for each word. **(5.7)**

1. graceful	→	without grace	full of grace
2. homeless	→	with a home	without a home
3. honorable	→	can honor	without honor
4. fearful	→	without fear	full of fear
5. useless	→	able to use	without use
6. bendable	→	not able to bend	able to bend
7. skillful	→	full of skill	without skill
8. careless	→	full of care	without care
9. beautiful	→	without beauty	full of beauty
10. speechless	→	able to speak	without speech

Copyright 2006 Growing With Grammar Level 4. All Rights Reserved

C. Underline the main **verbs** once and the **helping verbs** twice. **(4.7)**

1. Joshua has been practicing the piano.
2. You could have fed the ducks at the pond.
3. Did you bring your book?
4. Jack should have flossed his teeth.
5. Quentin might be walking to your house.

D. These **directions** are not in the correct order. Rewrite them so that the directions make sense. **(3.11)**

How to Scramble Eggs

Then put the egg in a pan.
Third, beat the egg with an eggbeater.
First, crack the eggshell and empty the egg into a bowl.
Finally, cook the egg until it is done.
Second, add salt and pepper.

Copyright 2006 Growing With Grammar Level 4. All Rights Reserved

Worksheet 5.8 (Building Sentences with Adjectives) Name____________________

A. Rewrite these sentences. Make them more interesting by answering the questions in parentheses with **adjectives**. **(5.8)**

Example: I bought apples. → (How many apples?) (What kind of apples?)
I bought **three red** apples.

1. Uncle caught fish. → (Whose uncle?) (How many fish?)

____

2. Boys jumped in the lake. → (How many boys?) (Which lake?)

____

3. This is a house. → (Whose house?) (What kind of house?)

____

4. Pie and cake were served. → (What kind of pie?) (What kind of cake?)

____

5. The shoes match the dress. → (Whose shoes?) (Which dress?)

____

6. Grandfather ate a peach. → (Whose Grandfather?) (What kind of peach?)

____

7. Car needs tires. → (Which car?) (How many tires?)

____

8. Flowers are from Ted. → (Which flowers?) (What kind of flowers?)

____

Copyright 2006 Growing With Grammar Level 4. All Rights Reserved

B. Write the comparative and superlative forms of these **adjectives**. **(5.6)**

1. good ______________________ ______________________
2. bad ______________________ ______________________
3. many ______________________ ______________________
4. much ______________________ ______________________
5. little ______________________ ______________________
6. mean ______________________ ______________________
7. fast ______________________ ______________________
8. playful ______________________ ______________________
9. warm ______________________ ______________________
10. considerate ______________________ ______________________
11. thoughtful ______________________ ______________________
12. pleasant ______________________ ______________________
13. short ______________________ ______________________
14. sweet ______________________ ______________________
15. high ______________________ ______________________

C. Underline the **verb phrase** for each sentence. **(4.8)**

1. We have skied for three hours.
2. Veronica did not finish her work carefully.
3. You should have gone to bed sooner.
4. The children were watching a ball game.
5. I am not sleeping.

Copyright 2006 Growing With Grammar Level 4. All Rights Reserved

Worksheet 5.9 (Writing Friendly Letters and Postcards) Name____________________

A. Write the names of the parts of this **letter** on the lines below. **(5.9)**

1. ____________________ 567 Main Street
Baltimore, MD 21075
June 1, 20--

2. ____________________ Dear Grandma,

3. ____________________ I won first prize at the science fair! I cannot wait for you to come visit us so I can show you the ribbon I won. Mom said she would take a picture of me with my science fair project to send to you.

I hope I get to see you soon! Give Grandpa a hug for me.

4. ____________________ Love,

5. ____________________ Julie

B. Write each **letter part** correctly using proper **capitalization** and **punctuation**. **(5.9)**

1. yours truly ____________________
2. dear mrs. Gordon ____________________
3. san Antonio TX ____________________
4. october 23 20-- ____________________
5. sincerely ____________________
6. dear Jonathan ____________________
7. 135 cooper St. ____________________
8. march 5 20-- ____________________
9. your friend ____________________
10. 1300 barnett Avenue ____________________
11. bakersfield, ca 93301 ____________________
12. dear uncle Bill ____________________

Copyright 2006 Growing With Grammar Level 4. All Rights Reserved

C. Write your own **postcard**. Pretend that you are on vacation with your family and you are writing to your best friend. Include your friend's address. **(5.9)**

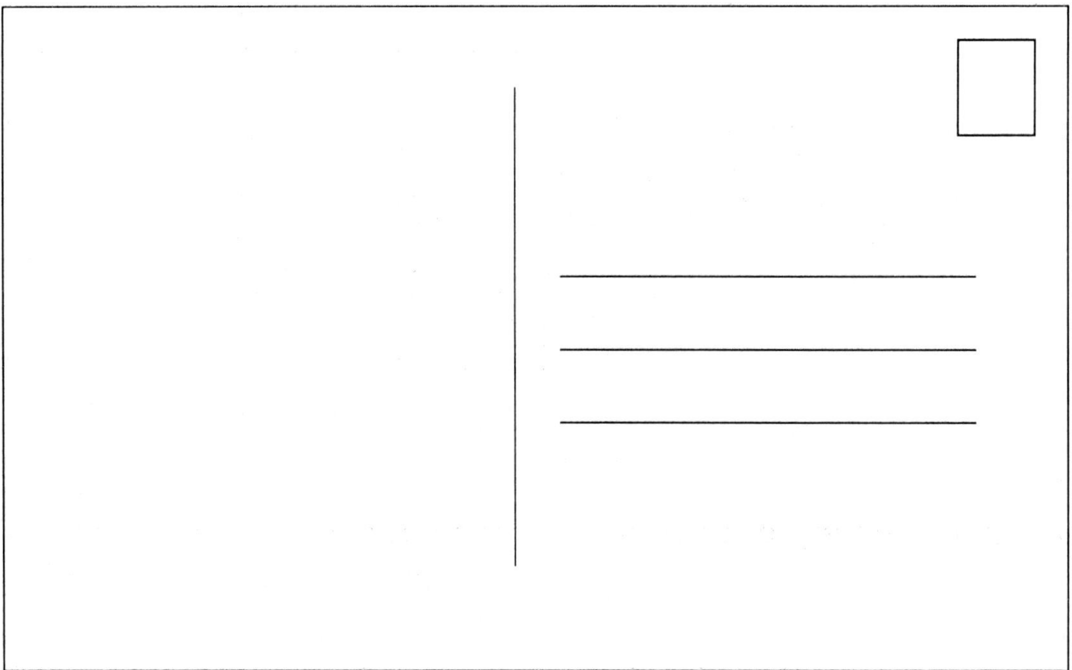

D. **Diagram** these sentences. **(1.4, 4.2, 4.4, & 5.2)**

1. Several white swans were flying.
2. The second boy is my older cousin.
3. A small girl ate a large hot pizza.
4. Dad's new car was a red convertible.

Copyright 2006 Growing With Grammar Level 4. All Rights Reserved

Worksheet 5.10 (Writing Business Letters) Name_______________________

A. Underline the 17 words that should be capitalized in this **business letter**. **(5.10)**

357 tree street
charleston, SC 29401
january 21, 20--

mr. raymond brown
brown toy Company
246 main Avenue
columbia, SC 29201

dear Mr. brown:

i would like to find out more information on your new toy line. please send me a brochure of the toys available. I heard about them from a clerk at my local store. Would you also please tell me where I can buy one?

sincerely,

John Harris
John harris

B. Write the names of the parts of this **business letter** on the lines below. **(5.10)**

1. _______________________ Route 5
Minneapolis, MN 55199
March 1, 20--

2. _______________________ Roger Boyle
Boyle's Skateboards
333 Skating Rd.
Morton, IL 61550

3. _______________________ Dear Mr. Boyle:

4. _______________________ I would like to order a catalog of your new skateboard models. I have enclosed a check for $5.00 to cover the cost of the catalog and postage.

5. _______________________ Best regards,

6. _______________________ Tommy Johnson
Tommy Johnson

Copyright 2006 Growing With Grammar Level 4. All Rights Reserved

C. Answer the questions below by writing <u>**F**</u> for friendly letter, <u>**B**</u> for business letter, or <u>**P**</u> for post card. **(5.9 & 5.10)**

1. _____ What type of note do people often send to friends or family when they are on vacation?

2. _____ What type of letter has an inside address?

3. _____ What type of letter would you write to order a product?

4. _____ What type of letter has five parts and is a personal letter?

5. _____ What type of letter has a colon after the greeting?

6. _____ What type of letter has six parts?

7. _____ What type of note is a quick way to let someone know you are having a good time?

8. _____ What type of letter would you write to a friend that includes information about yourself?

D. Underline the **adjectives** in each sentence. **(5.1)**

1. Two red birds built this large nest.
2. Mike's green iguana ate that small insect.
3. That third boy is my friend.
4. Many families visit this luxurious hotel.
5. Those people sold their old car.
6. My older brother bought that expensive new coat.
7. George caught five large fish.
8. Several students lost their new books.
9. That friendly woman brought some delicious food.
10. We purchased that large blue house.

Copyright 2006 Growing With Grammar Level 4. All Rights Reserved

Worksheet 5.11 (Other Types of Social Notes) Name____________________

A. What type of **note** would you write for each occasion listed? Write **thank you letter** or **invitation** on the lines. **(5.11)**

1. Your friend gave you a gift for your birthday. ____________________
2. Your family is having a cookout. ____________________
3. Your Grandma taught you how to sew. ____________________
4. Your neighbor helped mow the lawn when you were ill. ____________________
5. You are having a surprise party for your mother. ____________________
6. You are having an ice skating party. ____________________

B. Write a **thank you letter** for a gift you have recently received. Remember to mention the gift. **(5.11)**

Copyright 2006 Growing With Grammar Level 4. All Rights Reserved

C. Write each **letter part** correctly using proper **capitalization** and **punctuation**. **(5.9 - 5.11)**

1. sincerely yours ______________________
2. dear mr. jones: ______________________
3. best regards ______________________
4. 210 washington st. ______________________
5. november 6, 20-- ______________________
6. dear madam ______________________
7. denver co 80206 ______________________
8. your niece ______________________
9. dear aunt Milly ______________________
10. jeffrey ______________________

D. Write the correct **past tense** for the **verb** in parentheses. **(4.11)**

1. Dane (break) his glasses yesterday. ______________
2. My puppy (grow) into a large dog. ______________
3. We have (eat) the entire pizza. ______________
4. The boys (catch) many fireflies last night. ______________
5. We (make) cookies yesterday. ______________
6. Alex (buy) a gift for his sister. ______________
7. I have (ride) that horse five times. ______________
8. Have you (see) the new exhibit at the museum? ______________
9. Steve (spend) his money on candy. ______________
10. She has (write) to her pen pal. ______________

Copyright 2006 Growing With Grammar Level 4. All Rights Reserved

Worksheet 5.12 (Addressing an Envelope) Name______________________________

A. Address this **envelope**. Write your own name and address as the **return address**. Use the address below for the **mailing address**. **(5.12)**

Mailing address: J. Johnson
488 Patterson Avenue
New York NY 10002

____

____

____

Stamp

____

____

____

B. Rewrite these sentences. Make them more interesting by answering the questions in parentheses with **adjectives**. **(5.8)**

1. Cat caught the mouse. → (Whose cat?) (What kind of mouse?)

____

2. Birds were in the nest. → (How many birds?) (Which nest?)

____

3. The ball was in the box. → (Whose ball?) (What kind of box?)

____

4. A snake slithers near the rock. → (What kind of snake?) (What kind of rock?)

____

Copyright 2006 Growing With Grammar Level 4. All Rights Reserved

C. Underline the **adjectives** in each sentence. **(5.1)**

1. My big brother crashed his new black bike.
2. Some turtles have soft shells.
3. Those two large apples fell from Bob's tall tree.
4. Have you seen my sister?
5. That sleepy child is crying.
6. This little girl is wearing pretty pink shoes.
7. Marie's red truck hit this huge tree.
8. That dog has many sharp teeth.

D. **Diagram** these sentences. **(1.4, 1.6, 4.2, 4.4, & 5.2)**

1. This red flower is a rose.

2. This jacket matches those pants.

3. Those two girls are my friends.

4. Joe and Ed painted the old barn.

Copyright 2006 Growing With Grammar Level 4. All Rights Reserved

Chapter 5 Review

Name________________________

A. Write **Whose**, **Which One**, **How Many**, or **What Kind** to tell what type of **adjective** is in bold. **(5.1)**

1. A **chocolate** cake is in the oven. ______________________
2. Bryan dropped **two** glasses. ______________________
3. Jerome made **that** mess. ______________________
4. **Your** shoe is untied. ______________________
5. Is that his **second** helping? ______________________

B. Circle the correct **order of adjectives** in the following sentences. **(5.1)**

1. That is an (old wooden) (wooden old) spoon.
2. We saw a (black large) (large black) dog.
3. The boys picked (round red) (red round) tomatoes.

C. Circle the correct **articles** to complete these sentences. **(5.1)**

1. (An, A) clown juggled balls for (a, the) children.
2. (An, The) bear went into (a, an) underground cave.
3. Craig found (a, an) egg that fell out of (a , an) nest.

D. Circle the correct word for each sentence. **(5.3)**

1. (These, This) picnic table is ours.
2. Is (that, those) an apple tree?
3. (These, This) pearls were found inside oysters.
4. Mom planted (that, those) flowers last week.

E. Change these proper nouns into **proper adjectives**. Check the dictionary if you are unsure of the spelling. **(5.4)**

1. Spain ____________________ 3. America ____________________

2. Russia ____________________ 4. Austria ____________________

Copyright 2006 Growing With Grammar Level 4. All Rights Reserved

F. Circle the correct form of the **adjective** for each sentence. **(5.5)**

1. Your idea is (good, better) than my idea.
2. Audra has a (smallest, smaller) bike than Kyra.
3. That is the (most beautiful, beautifulest) rainbow I have ever seen.
4. Your dad is the (taller, tallest) man in our neighborhood.
5. Sheila has (more, most) chores today than yesterday.
6. This is the (bad, worst) song I have ever heard.

G. Write the **comparative** and **superlative** forms of these **adjectives**. **(5.6)**

Examples: wide → wider widest
curious → more curious most curious

1. soft ______________________ ______________________
2. much ______________________ ______________________
3. fantastic ______________________ ______________________
4. good ______________________ ______________________
5. little ______________________ ______________________
6. funny ______________________ ______________________
7. bad ______________________ ______________________
8. fast ______________________ ______________________
9. many ______________________ ______________________
10. colorful ______________________ ______________________

H. Circle the correct meaning for each word. **(5.7)**

1. readable → able to be read not able to be read
2. cheerful → full of cheer without cheer
3. comfortable → without comfort able to comfort
4. pointless → with a point without a point
5. beautiful → without beauty full of beauty

Copyright 2006 Growing With Grammar Level 4. All Rights Reserved

I. Rewrite these sentences. Make them more interesting by answering the questions in parentheses with **adjectives**. **(5.8)**

Example: I bought apples. ⟶ (How many apples?) (What kind of apples?)

I bought **three red** apples.

1. Chipmunks gathered nuts. → (What kind of chipmunks?) (How many nuts?)

____

2. Cat caught a mouse. → (Whose cat?) (Which mouse?)

____

3. A dog watched boys. → (What kind of dog?) (Which boys?)

____

J. Write the name of each **letter part**. **(5.9)**

1. Dear Cassandra, ____________________
2. Stephanie ____________________
3. 101 Miami St.
Clermont, FL
June 5, 20-- ____________________
4. Sincerely, ____________________
5. I think we will be great pen pals. How do you like living in Florida? Write soon! ____________________

K. Write each **letter part** correctly using proper **capitalization** and **punctuation**. **(5.9)**

1. dear mr. mano ____________________
2. 234 holiday Rd. ____________________
3. best regards ____________________
4. december 3 20-- ____________________
5. your friend ____________________
6. dear ronny ____________________

Copyright 2006 Growing With Grammar Level 4. All Rights Reserved

L. Address this **envelope**. Write your own name and address as the **return address**. Use the address below for the **mailing address**.

Mailing address: B. James
900 Richard Ave.
Las Vegas NV 89044

M. **Diagram** these sentences. **(1.4, 1.7, 4.2, 4.4, & 5.2)**

1. The alert officer yelled and whistled.
2. Those two girls are my good friends.
3. The second man is my uncle.
4. The brown cat had climbed our old tree.

Copyright 2006 Growing With Grammar Level 4. All Rights Reserved

Worksheet 6.1 (Adverbs) Name________________________

A. Write **How**, **When**, or **Where** to tell what type of **adverb** is in bold. **(6.1)**

1. Francesca yelled **loudly**. ________________
2. You should go **outside** to play. ________________
3. The boys went **upstairs**. ________________
4. The fish swam **quickly**. ________________
5. **Today** we visited the zoo. ________________
6. The sun shines **brightly**. ________________
7. **Tonight** the play begins. ________________
8. I saw the shark **first**. ________________
9. A butterfly flew **past**. ________________
10. Katie looked **up**. ________________
11. I spoke too **hastily**. ________________
12. We arrived **yesterday**. ________________
13. Jason runs **fast**. ________________
14. He wants to eat **now**. ________________
15. The lion ran **swiftly**. ________________
16. My dog **easily** catches a ball. ________________
17. Come **here**. ________________
18. **Now** I hear it. ________________
19. **Tomorrow** he comes for dinner. ________________
20. Do your work **efficiently**. ________________

Copyright 2006 Growing With Grammar Level 4. All Rights Reserved

B. Write the **verb** or **verb phrase** on the line that the **adverb** in bold describes. **(6.1)**

Example: We went **downstairs**. → went

1. The boys **always** eat dessert. ____________________
2. Avery whispered **softly**. ____________________
3. Gordon lives **nearby**. ____________________
4. We play tennis **frequently**. ____________________
5. John is leaving **now**. ____________________
6. The dog walked **slowly**. ____________________
7. My mother works **hard**. ____________________
8. Did you look **there**? ____________________

C. Rewrite these sentences. Make them more interesting by answering the questions in parentheses with **adverbs**. **(6.1)**

Example: I found a quarter. → (When?)

Yesterday I found a quarter.

1. Take the dog. → (Where?)

____

2. The children play. → (How?)

____

3. We saw an eagle. → (When?)

____

4. The crowd looked. → (Where?)

____

5. Frogs leap. → (How?)

____

Copyright 2006 Growing With Grammar Level 4. All Rights Reserved

Worksheet 6.2 (Diagramming Adverbs) Name____________________________

A. **Diagram** these sentences. **(1.4, 1.12, 4.2, 4.4, & 6.2)**

1. Ann yelled loudly.

2. Cindy left today.

3. Where are you going?

4. The lion ran swiftly.

5. Brady behaved rudely.

6. When will you arrive?

7. We ate lunch quickly.

8. Katie looked up.

Copyright 2006 Growing With Grammar Level 4. All Rights Reserved

B. Underline the **adverb** in each sentence. On the line, write the question the adverb answers: **How**, **Where**, or **When**. **(6.1)**

1. The crowd cheers wildly. ____________________
2. We will sit there. ____________________
3. I saw Jennifer first. ____________________
4. Where did the bird go? ____________________
5. He eagerly drank the water. ____________________
6. We sometimes have a picnic. ____________________
7. Don't go far. ____________________
8. When will you eat dinner? ____________________
9. Adriana will arrive soon. ____________________
10. How did the grasshopper jump? ____________________

C. In each sentence, the verb is underlined. On the line, write the **adverb** that describes the verb. **(6.1)**

1. Today we are learning classical music. ____________________
2. Karen slept soundly on the couch. ____________________
3. You should study your math facts now. ____________________
4. The boys drank lemonade outside. ____________________
5. My sister will be selling tickets tonight for the play. ____________________
6. Alexander left early. ____________________
7. The swimmer practices often. ____________________
8. We met our friends there. ____________________

Copyright 2006 Growing With Grammar Level 4. All Rights Reserved

Worksheet 6.3 (Adverb Placement) Name______________________________

A. Underline the **adverb** in each sentence. **(6.3)**

1. Softly the children whispered.
2. The girls loudly laughed.
3. The boys played quietly.
4. We visited our cousins yesterday.
5. Today we see our grandmother.
6. We often play with our friends.
7. The rain fell outside.
8. Down came the snow.
9. Lori wraps the package carefully.
10. Joe securely seals the box.
11. Eagerly she opens the mail.
12. They will leave soon.
13. Now the movie starts.
14. We always play in the snow.
15. Usually we feed the birds.
16. My family wakes early.
17. Hawks can see sharply.
18. The wind gently blows.
19. Joanne lives nearby.
20. Where is your hat?

B. Rewrite each word as an **adverb**. **(6.1)**

Example: smooth → ____smooth**ly**____

1. careful ______________________
2. quiet ______________________
3. tight ______________________
4. rapid ______________________
5. playful ______________________
6. slow ______________________
7. sharp ______________________
8. bold ______________________
9. glad ______________________
10. eager ______________________

C. Rewrite these sentences. Make them more interesting by answering the questions in parentheses with **adverbs**. **(6.1)**

Example: I found a quarter. → (When?)

Yesterday I found a quarter.

1 Music plays. → (When?)

____

2. The rain fell. → (Where?)

____

Copyright 2006 Growing With Grammar Level 4. All Rights Reserved

D. **Diagram** these sentences. **(1.4, 1.7, 1.12, 4.2, 4.4, 5.2, 6.2)**

1. The red birds sang beautifully.

2. Selma and Mara ran quickly outside.

3. Softly the children whispered.

4. How did the girls laugh?

5. You should leave now.

6. Now my sister is working hard.

7. When did the boys play?

8. Where did the rain fall?.

Copyright 2006 Growing With Grammar Level 4. All Rights Reserved

Worksheet 6.4 (Adverbs that Compare) Name______________________

A. Write the comparative and superlative forms of these **adverbs**. **(6.4)**

Examples: hard → harder hardest
gracefully → more gracefully most gracefully

1. well ______________ ______________
2. heavily ______________ ______________
3. badly ______________ ______________
4. fast ______________ ______________
5. far ______________ ______________
6. slowly ______________ ______________
7. little ______________ ______________
8. carefully ______________ ______________
9. easily ______________ ______________
10. suddenly ______________ ______________
11. smoothly ______________ ______________
12. brightly ______________ ______________
13. coldly ______________ ______________
14. quickly ______________ ______________
15. sharply ______________ ______________
16. loudly ______________ ______________
17. softly ______________ ______________
18. quietly ______________ ______________

Copyright 2006 Growing With Grammar Level 4. All Rights Reserved

B. Circle the correct form of the **adverb** for each sentence. **(6.4)**

1. This car runs (fast, faster, fastest) than that car.
2. I feel (badly, worse, worst) today than I did yesterday.
3. She stayed up the (late, later, latest) of everyone.
4. Bob swings (carefully, more carefully, most carefully) of all the boys.
5. The blue kite flies (high, higher, highest) than the green kite.
6. Jackie spent (little, less, least) on her lunch than Claudia.
7. Dan's car is the (most slowest, slowest) in town.
8. Our group walked (fast, faster, fastest) of all the groups.
9. Dad works (hard, harder, hardest) on the weekends than the weekdays.
10. Terrence remembers the song (well, better, best) of all the singers.

C. Rewrite these sentences using proper **capitalization** and **punctuation.**
(1.11, 2.9, & 3.7 - 3.10)

1. john did you visit the grand canyon

____

2. cameron brushed his hair but I flossed my teeth

____

3. aunt patricia used ajax cleanser in the sink

____

4. robert can you locate saskatchewan on the map

____

Copyright 2006 Growing With Grammar Level 4. All Rights Reserved

Worksheet 6.5 (Relative Pronouns and Relative Adverbs) Name____________________________

A. Underline the **relative pronoun** or **relative adverb** in each sentence. Write the noun it tells more about on the line. **(6.5)**

1. There must be a reason why the baby is crying. ____________________________
2. Tomorrow is the day when vacation starts. ____________________________
3. Joe is a person whose opinions are usually reliable. ____________________________
4. The boy who won the contest is my cousin. ____________________________
5. This is the park where I met my friend Jill. ____________________________
6. The shoes that Bobby wore were new. ____________________________

B. Circle the correct **relative pronoun** or **relative adverb** for each sentence. **(6.5)**

1. The book (who, that) I wanted to purchase was gone.
2. Mr. William is the man (who, whose) helped me with physics.
3. What is the reason (when, why) you didn't finish your school work?
4. The day (why, when) we went to the park was fun.
5. He is the man (that, whose) restaurant closed last week.
6. This is the museum (why, where) I first met Tommy.

Copyright 2006 Growing With Grammar Level 4. All Rights Reserved

C. Circle the correct form of the **adverb** for each sentence. **(6.4)**

1. The water flows (faster, fastest) today than yesterday.
2. Bryce jumped (higher, highest) of all the boys on the team.
3. Mrs. Jones drives (carefully, more carefully) than Mr. Brown.
4. Beth sings (better, best) than Tom.
5. Mike can set up a tent (more quickly, most quickly) than I can.
6. Vanessa learns music (easily, more easily) than other people.
7. Nelson plays tennis (better, best) of any person in town.
8. My plants grow (worse, worst) in the shade than in the sunlight.

D. **Diagram** these sentences. **(1.4, 1.7, 4.2, 4.4, 5.2, 6.2)**

1. Rain and hail fell down quickly.
2. Mia sings well.
3. My friend was riding her bike carefully.
4. When did your package arrive?

Copyright 2006 Growing With Grammar Level 4. All Rights Reserved

Worksheet 6.6 (Double Negatives) Name______________________________

A. Circle the correct word to complete each sentence. **(6.6)**

1. Mom said that we (can, can't) not go to the pool.
2. I don't want (no, any) ice cream with my cake.
3. Marianne doesn't (never, ever) watch television.
4. There (is, isn't) no gas in the gas tank.
5. We didn't see (anybody, nobody) at the park.
6. The girls aren't going (anywhere, nowhere) today.
7. They won't take (anybody, nobody) with them.
8. She has not written to (any, none) of her friends.
9. Our cat never has (no, any) fleas.
10. I am not doing (nothing, anything).
11. She won't tell (nobody, anybody).
12. I (can, can't) hear nothing when I wear earplugs.
13. Whitney doesn't want (nothing, anything) to eat.
14. Roger hasn't (never, ever) been on a rollercoaster.
15. He doesn't call us (no more, anymore).
16. I don't want (no, any) broccoli.
17. You never said (anything, nothing).
18. She doesn't have (any, no) excuse.
19. He has never done (nothing, anything) to help her.
20. She didn't play with (no one, anyone) at the pool.

Copyright 2006 Growing With Grammar Level 4. All Rights Reserved

B. Rewrite these sentences. Answer the questions after each sentence to make them more interesting by adding **adjectives** and **adverbs**. **(5.8 & 6.5)**

Example: Mother searched. → (**Whose** mother?) (**Where** did Mother search?)

My mother searched **everywhere**.

1. The rabbit jumped. → (What kind of rabbit?) (Where did the rabbit jump?)

____

2. Rain fell. → (What kind of rain?) (Where did rain fall?)

____

3. The boy shouted. → (Which boy?) (How did the boy shout?)

____

4. The team played. → (Which team?) (Where did the team play?)

____

5. The game is over. → (Whose game?) (When is the game over?)

____

6. Students saw a movie. → (How many students?) (Which movie?)

____

7. A child cried. → (What kind of child?) (How did the child cry?)

____

8. Sue purchased books. → (How many books?) (When did she purchase books?)

____

Copyright 2006 Growing With Grammar Level 4. All Rights Reserved

Worksheet 6.7 (Synonyms and Antonyms) Name______________________________

A. Write a **synonym** for each word. **(6.7)**

1. happy ______________________________
2. damp ______________________________
3. scream ______________________________
4. thin ______________________________
5. huge ______________________________
6. quick ______________________________
7. loud ______________________________
8. laugh ______________________________
9. sleepy ______________________________
10. raise ______________________________

B. Write an **antonym** for each word. **(6.7)**

1. happy ______________________________
2. damp ______________________________
3. scream ______________________________
4. thin ______________________________
5. huge ______________________________
6. quick ______________________________
7. loud ______________________________
8. laugh ______________________________
9. sleepy ______________________________
10. raise ______________________________

Copyright 2006 Growing With Grammar Level 4. All Rights Reserved

C. For each set of words, write **A** if they are **antonyms** and **S** if they are **synonyms**. **(6.7)**

1. _____ top / bottom
2. _____ first / last
3. _____ close / shut
4. _____ loan / borrow
5. _____ live / die
6. _____ frighten / scare
7. _____ end / finish
8. _____ job / task
9. _____ right / correct
10. _____ same / alike
11. _____ push / pull
12. _____ short / brief
13. _____ terrible / awful
14. _____ exciting / boring
15. _____ open / close
16. _____ assist / help

D. **Diagram** these sentences. **(1.4, 1.12, 4.2, 4.4, 5.2, 6.2, 6.6)**

1. The young boy was not running quickly.
2. The beautiful woman is my aunt.
3. Where did you eat your lunch?
4. The girls were not doing their chores.

Copyright 2006 Growing With Grammar Level 4. All Rights Reserved

Worksheet 6.8 (Homonyms) Name____________________________

A. Write a **homonym** for each word. **(6.8)**

1. knot ____________________
2. son ____________________
3. won ____________________
4. your ____________________
5. flew ____________________
6. aunt ____________________
7. their ____________________
8. dew ____________________
9. bawl ____________________
10. brake ____________________
11. fare ____________________
12. seen ____________________
13. write ____________________
14. hear ____________________

B. Circle the correct **homonyms** for each sentence. **(6.8)**

1. Joe (flu, flew) off his chair when he (heard, herd) the loud noise.
2. (Our, Hour) little sister is (to, too, two) years old.
3. Father used the (acts, ax) to chop (wood, would).
4. Please (chews, choose) the (clothes, close) you want to (by, buy).
5. (Do, Dew) you (knead, need) a new (pear, pair, pare) of jeans?
6. The dog wagged its (tale, tail) when it (knew, new) we were home.

Copyright 2006 Growing With Grammar Level 4. All Rights Reserved

C. For each set of words, write A if they are **antonyms**, S if they are **synonyms**, or H if they are **homonyms**. **(6.7 & 6.8)**

1. _____ borrow / loan
2. _____ dark / light
3. _____ ore / or
4. _____ jump / leap
5. _____ least / most
6. _____ their / there
7. _____ waste / waist
8. _____ injure / damage

D. These **directions** are not in the correct order. Rewrite them so they make sense. **(3.11)**

How to Wash the Dishes

Then wash the dishes in the soapy water.
First fill the sink with warm water.
Finally dry the dishes with a clean towel.
Next add dishwashing soap.

____

____

____

____

____

____

____

____

____

____

____

____

Copyright 2006 Growing With Grammar Level 4. All Rights Reserved

Worksheet 6.9 (Using Good and Well) Name____________________________

A. Circle the correct word. **(6.9)**

1. She did (good, well) work.
2. That was a (good, well) book.
3. Did you sleep (good, well)?
4. I don't feel (good, well) today.
5. Travis throws (good, well).
6. You made a (good, well) cherry pie.
7. Jamie cannot hear (good, well).
8. This is a (good, well) movie.
9. Georgia's grades are (good, well).
10. You did (good, well) on your tests.
11. Is Jackie feeling (good, well) today?
12. You should eat (good, well) food.

B. Write **good** or **well** to complete each sentence. **(6.9)**

1. Rebecca is ____________________________ at multiplication.
2. Marie always does her work ____________________________.
3. Jackson is a ____________________________ dancer.
4. Bill sings very ____________________________.
5. Paul speaks ____________________________.
6. We had a ____________________________ day.
7. How did you do that so ____________________________ ?
8. None of us had ____________________________ luck.

Copyright 2006 Growing With Grammar Level 4. All Rights Reserved

C. Write a **homonym**, **synonym**, and **antonym** for each word. **(6.7 & 6.8)**

	Homonym	Synonym	Antonym
1. right	________	________	________
2. bawl	________	________	________
3. break	________	________	________
4. great	________	________	________
5. threw	________	________	________
6. close	________	________	________
7. pair	________	________	________
8. seize	________	________	________

D. **Diagram** these sentences. **(1.4, 1.12, 4.2, 4.4, 5.2, 6.2, 6.6)**

1. Muriel and Shanna make tasty bread.

2. Run fast!

3. Marco quickly ate his greasy pizza.

4. Where is her blue sweater?

Copyright 2006 Growing With Grammar Level 4. All Rights Reserved

Worksheet 6.10 (Writing a Descriptive Paragraph) Name________________________

A. Below are four **topic sentences**. Write a **descriptive paragraph** about one of these sentences. Be sure to make the topic sentence you choose the first sentence of your paragraph. Write two or three more sentences that include specific details about your topic. Include adjectives and adverbs to make your description seem real. Describe the sights, smells, tastes, sounds, and feel of your topic. **(6.10)**

1. My favorite breakfast is ______________________.
2. My favorite flavor of ice cream is______________________.
3. ______________________ is my favorite season.
4. The best vacation I have ever taken was ______________________.

Copyright 2006 Growing With Grammar Level 4. All Rights Reserved

B. Write **good** or **well** to complete each sentence. **(6.9)**

1. Are you feeling ______________________________?
2. Kim is a ______________________________ pitcher.
3. Is she having a ______________________________ day?
4. My shoes fit ______________________________.
5. This is a ______________________________ song.

C. For each set of words, write **A** if they are **antonyms**, **S** if they are **synonyms**, or **H** if they are **homonyms**. **(6.7 & 6.8)**

1. _____ our / hour
2. _____ long / brief
3. _____ clean / dirty
4. _____ close / clothes
5. _____ deer / dear
6. _____ fight / argue
7. _____ pretty / ugly
8. _____ some / sum
9. _____ large / enormous
10. _____ present / gift
11. _____ bear / bare
12. _____ in / out
13. _____ kind / nice
14. _____ pail / pale
15. _____ light / heavy
16. _____ fast / swift

D. Add **quotation marks** to these sentences. Underline the **speaker tags**. **(1.15)**

1. Kelsey said, I have a new puppy.
2. Are you going to the museum? asked Micah.
3. I snorkeled for the first time! exclaimed Wyatt.
4. The rain is falling softly, said Mom.
5. Helen asked, Are your shoes waterproof?

Copyright 2006 Growing With Grammar Level 4. All Rights Reserved

Chapter 6 Review

Name____________________________

A. Write **How**, **When**, or **Where** to tell what type of **adverb** is in bold. **(6.1)**

1. The exhibit opened **yesterday**. ____________________
2. You learn **quickly**. ____________________
3. Your jacket is **upstairs**. ____________________
4. He will be home **later**. ____________________
5. Jorge **carefully** stepped over the broken glass. ____________________
6. Jeff waited **impatiently**. ____________________

B. Write the comparative and superlative forms of these **adverbs**. **(6.4)**

Examples: high → higher highest
heavily → more heavily most heavily

1. far ____________________ ____________________
2. loudly ____________________ ____________________
3. badly ____________________ ____________________
4. skillfully ____________________ ____________________
5. hard ____________________ ____________________
6. proudly ____________________ ____________________

C. Circle the correct **relative pronoun** or **relative adverb** for each sentence. **(6.5)**

1. The man (which, who) came to the movie was my uncle.
2. Do you know the reason (when, why) so many people are sick?
3. This is the place (why, where) my parents were married.
4. The book (that, whose) I got from the library is due today.

Copyright 2006 Growing With Grammar Level 4. All Rights Reserved

D. Circle the correct word to complete each sentence. **(6.6)**

1. We haven't (never, ever) been to New York.
2. Johnny does not ever do (no, any) work.
3. It doesn't make (any, no) difference to him.
4. I looked for cookies, but there weren't (any, none).
5. Didn't he ever do (anything, nothing) about that?
6. This doesn't make (no, any) sense to me.

E. For each set of words, write **A** if they are **antonyms**, **S** if they are **synonyms**, or **H** if they are **homonyms**. **(6.7 & 6.8)**

1. _____ here / hear
2. _____ walk / run
3. _____ to / two
4. _____ first / last
5. _____ sit / stand
6. _____ ate / eight
7. _____ begin / start
8. _____ right / left
9. _____ missed / mist
10. _____ dear / deer
11. _____ early / late
12. _____ rob / steal

F. Circle the correct word. **(6.9)**

1. This is a (good, well) fishing spot.
2. How did you do that so (good, well)?
3. The steak we had for dinner was (good, well).
4. Kara writes (good, well).
5. Are you feeling (good, well)?
6. Tennis is a (good, well) sport.

Copyright 2006 Growing With Grammar Level 4. All Rights Reserved

G. **Diagram** these sentences. **(1.4, 1.12, 4.2, 4.4, 5.2, 6.2, 6.6)**

1. The children happily painted their pictures.
2. How will he learn the poem?
3. My friend did not sing beautifully.
4. Does the car have new brakes?

Copyright 2006 Growing With Grammar Level 4. All Rights Reserved

Copyright 2006 Growing With Grammar Level 4. All Rights Reserved

Worksheet 7.1 (Prepositions) Name____________________________

A. In each sentence, underline the **preposition** once and underline the **object of the preposition** twice. **(7.1)**

1. Jerry jumped into the water.
2. Aisha rode her bicycle around the block.
3. Did you look underneath the couch?
4. The boy gazed at the birds.
5. A rabbit hopped under the porch.
6. Let's go to the beach.
7. Harry reached across the table.
8. The bird stays in the cage.
9. Charmaine lives with her grandmother.
10. The spider crawled through the window.
11. Jolie works in the evenings.
12. This is a gift from my sister.

B. Write the first column of **prepositions** from lesson **7.1**. **(7.1)**

____

____

____

____

____

____

____

____

____

____

Copyright 2006 Growing With Grammar Level 4. All Rights Reserved

C. Add words after each preposition to complete these sentences. Underline the **preposition** once and the **object of the preposition** twice. **(7.1)**

Example: Our house is near → Our house is near **the lake**.

1. The boy hid behind ______________________________.
2. I ran around ______________________________.
3. She found the hamster under ______________________________.
4. We found shelter during ______________________________.
5. She was born in ______________________________.
6. They walked across ______________________________.
7. Will you sit with ______________________________?
8. Stuart went aboard ______________________________.

D. **Combine** or rewrite these sentences into one grammatically correct sentence that a) is either a compound sentence or b) includes either a **compound subject** or **compound predicate**. **(1.8 & 1.10)**

1. The nachos were prepared by Malcolm. The tacos were prepared by Malcolm.

____

2. Tracy went to the ticket booth. Tracy bought the tickets.

____

3. The boys left early. They got home late.

____

Copyright 2006 Growing With Grammar Level 4. All Rights Reserved

Worksheet 7.2 (Prepositional Phrases) Name__________________________

A. Draw a line under each **prepositional phrase**. Write the **preposition** on the line. **(7.2)**

1. The tree fell behind the house. __________________
2. The boulder rolled down the hill. __________________
3. The cat climbed up the tree. __________________
4. We went to the library. __________________
5. I saw a movie with Rosemary. __________________
6. The frog jumped in the river. __________________
7. Francine ran across the yard. __________________
8. I received a letter from my friend. __________________
9. I'll meet you at the bookstore. __________________
10. This package is from Bernard. __________________
11. My uncle is lying on the couch. __________________
12. The children played in the mud. __________________

B. Write the first column of **prepositions** from lesson **7.1**. **(7.1)**

____

____

____

____

____

____

____

____

____

____

Copyright 2006 Growing With Grammar Level 4. All Rights Reserved

C. Write sentences using the **prepositional phrases** below. **(7.2)**

1. into the house

____

2. through the yard

____

3. on the table

____

4. under the tree

____

5. before dinner

____

D. **Diagram** these sentences. **(1.4, 1.12, 4.2, 4.4, 5.2, 6.2, 6.6)**

1. The pirate did not find treasure.
3. The old donkey slowly pulled the red wagon.
2. When will you leave?
4. Ducks and geese fly quickly.

Copyright 2006 Growing With Grammar Level 4. All Rights Reserved

Worksheet 7.3 (Prepositional Phrase Used as an Adjective) Name____________________________

A. Underline the **adjective phrase**. Write the **noun** or **pronoun** it modifies on the line. (**Remember**, an adjective phrase **always** comes directly after the noun or pronoun it modifies.) **(7.3)**

1. The boy with blue eyes waved. ________________________
2. A bird near the fountain ate a worm. ________________________
3. The postcard in the mailbox is yours. ________________________
4. Those shoes on the porch are wet. ________________________
5. Dad bought a car with red paint. ________________________
6. Maria owns the house near the river. ________________________
7. The dog under the chair is scared. ________________________
8. The berries along the road are delicious. ________________________
9. I have a white dress with blue lace. ________________________
10. The woman across the street is my aunt. ________________________
11. Cakes with chocolate icing are my favorite dessert. ________________________
12. The marbles on the table are yours. ________________________

B. Write sentences using these **prepositional phrases** as **adjective phrases**. Underline the **noun** the phrase modifies. **(7.3)**

Example: in the barn → The <u>horse</u> **in the barn** ate the hay.

1. under the bed

____

2. on the counter

____

Copyright 2006 Growing With Grammar Level 4. All Rights Reserved

C. Write the second column of **prepositions** from lesson **7.1**. **(7.1)**

____

____

____

____

____

____

____

____

D. Rewrite these sentences with proper **capitalization** and **punctuation**. **(1.11, 3.7, 3.8, & 3.9)**

1. i spoke with mrs meyer on wednesday thomas

   ____

2. julie is your uncle myron a doctor

   ____

3. barney needs a ride from kennedy international airport

   ____

4. the tourists from ireland visited the hoover dam

   ____

5. the gibb family visited wailea beach in maui

   ____

Copyright 2006 Growing With Grammar Level 4. All Rights Reserved

Worksheet 7.4 (Prepositional Phrase Used as an Adverb) Name____________________

A. Underline each **adverb phrase** and write the **verb** it modifies on the line. (**Remember**, an adverb phrase can come at the **beginning** or the **end** of a sentence.) **(7.4)**

1. Meredith walked through the open door. ________________
2. The boys jumped off the diving board. ________________
3. We strolled around the lake. ________________
4. Fleur went home after the game. ________________
5. The girls played tag at the park. ________________
6. During the storm the dog barked. ________________
7. The children sang with great enthusiasm. ________________
8. Savannah left with her family. ________________
9. Into the forest the deer ran. ________________
10. Before the party we ate dinner. ________________
11. My aunt lives in the desert. ________________
12. The woman jogged toward the beach. ________________

B. Write sentences using these **prepositional phrases** as **adverb phrases**. Underline the **verb** the phrase modifies. **(7.4)**

Example: over a rock → Brady <u>jumped</u> **over a rock**.

1. through the water

____

2. up the steps

____

Copyright 2006 Growing With Grammar Level 4. All Rights Reserved

C. Write the **first** and **second** columns of **prepositions** from lesson **7.1**. **(7.1)**

Column 1	**Column 2**
______________	______________
______________	______________
______________	______________
______________	______________
______________	______________
______________	______________
______________	______________
______________	______________
______________	
______________	

D. Underline the **adjective phrase**. Write the **noun** or **pronoun** it modifies on the line. **(7.3)**

1. The man with the shovel is my father. ______________________
2. The boat on the beach is his. ______________________
3. We have a garden with many vegetables. ______________________
4. The book in the bag is yours. ______________________
5. The mural on the wall is beautiful. ______________________
6. That boy inside the candy store is my brother. ______________________
7. A woman aboard that boat caught three fish. ______________________
8. The gift from my brother is perfect! ______________________

E. In each sentence, underline the **preposition** once and underline the **object of the preposition** twice. **(7.1)**

1. Gregory sat by the steps.
2. We tied a hammock between two trees.
3. The light fell from the ceiling.
4. A lizard crawled over the leaves.
5. The girls went to the river.
6. My ring went down the drain.
7. The bird landed on the roof.
8. People of all ages attend the parade.

Copyright 2006 Growing With Grammar Level 4. All Rights Reserved

Worksheet 7.5 (Diagramming Prepositional Phrases) Name____________________________

A. **Diagram** these sentences with **adjective phrases**. **(1.4, 4.2, 4.4, 5.2, 6.2, & 7.5)**

1. The boy with blue eyes waved.
2. Maria owns the house near the river.
3. A woman aboard that boat caught a fish.
4. A bird near the fountain ate a worm.
5. Dad bought a car with red paint.
6. The boy inside the store is my brother.

Copyright 2006 Growing With Grammar Level 4. All Rights Reserved

B. **Diagram** these sentences with **adverb phrases**. **(1.4, 4.2, 4.4, 5.2, 6.2, & 7.5)**

1. We strolled around the lake.

2 . Savannah left with them.

3. My aunt lives in the desert.

4. During the storm the dog barked.

5. Into the forest the deer ran.

6. The woman jogged toward the beach.

Copyright 2006 Growing With Grammar Level 4. All Rights Reserved

Worksheet 7.6 (Preposition or Adverb) Name______________________

A. Write P if the word in bold is a **preposition**. Write A if it is an **adverb**. **Remember**: An **adverb** does **not** have an **object**. **(7.6)**

1. ________ Let the dog **inside**.
2. ________ **Inside** the cage the bird sat.
3. ________ A rock rolled **down** the hill.
4. ________ The building fell **down**.
5. ________ My sister stood **up**.
6. ________ **Up** the tree the cat climbed.
7. ________ Her umbrella was left **behind**.
8. ________ Carol hid **behind** the door.
9. ________ The boys camped **out**.
10. ________ Bryan dashed **out** the door.
11. ________ They heard a noise **in** the forest.
12. ________ Please come **in**.
13. ________ Look **around**.
14. ________ He went **around** the corner.
15. ________ Climb **aboard**.
16. ________ The boys went **aboard** the boat.
17. ________ The boys are **outside**.
18. ________ I see a butterfly **outside** the window.
19. ________ Joy fell **off** the swing.
20. ________ My hat fell **off**.

Copyright 2006 Growing With Grammar Level 4. All Rights Reserved

B. Write the **third** column of **prepositions** from lesson **7.1**. **(7.1)**

____

____

____

____

____

____

____

____

____

____

C. **Diagram** these sentences. **(1.4, 4.2, 4.4, 5.2, 6.2, & 7.5)**

1. The building fell down.

2. The children sang with great enthusiasm.

3. A rock rolled down the hill.

4. The boat on the beach is a canoe.

Copyright 2006 Growing With Grammar Level 4. All Rights Reserved

Worksheet 7.7 (Building Sentences with Prepositional Phrases) Name________________________

A. Rewrite each sentence and add a **prepositional phrase** to give more detail. (7.7)

Example: The boy raked leaves. → The boy **with brown hair** raked leaves.
-or- The boy raked leaves **into a pile**.

1. Kerry and I sat.

____

2. I saw a coyote.

____

3. The fish swam.

____

4. The street was filled.

____

5. Flowers add beauty.

____

6. Boats sail.

____

7. Birds fly.

____

8. Children play.

____

Copyright 2006 Growing With Grammar Level 4. All Rights Reserved

B. Write the **first**, **second**, and **third** columns of **prepositions** from lesson **7.1**. **(7.1)**

Column 1	Column 2	Column 3
____________	____________	____________
____________	____________	____________
____________	____________	____________
____________	____________	____________
____________	____________	____________
____________	____________	____________
____________	____________	____________
____________	____________	____________
____________		____________
____________		____________

C. Underline the **prepositional phrase**. Write the word that the phrase modifies on the line. **(7.4 & 7.3)**

1. The dog hid under the bed. ____________________
2. The dog with a red collar hid. ____________________
3. A boy raced down the road. ____________________
4. A boy in my neighborhood raced. ____________________
5. The letter from my sister arrived. ____________________
6. The letter arrived with the mail. ____________________
7. That girl in the blue sweater is my friend. ____________________
8. That girl moved to Alabama. ____________________
9. A cat with white paws ran. ____________________
10. A cat ran out the door. ____________________

Copyright 2006 Growing With Grammar Level 4. All Rights Reserved

Worksheet 7.8 (Conjunctions) Name_______________________

A. Underline any **conjunction** in these sentences. **(7.8)**

1. The wall was cracked, but now it is fixed.
2. Beetles and bees have wings.
3. The children and dogs ran through the fields.
4. Frank walked to the store, but his brother stayed home.
5. Girls or boys are allowed to enter the contest.
6. Herve sang, and his brother played the piano.
7. She raises chickens but not pigs.
8. Do you want to go to a movie or rent a video?

B. Complete each of the following sentences with the conjunctions **but** or **or**. **(7.8)**

1. You can drink soda __________ tea.
2. Jeremy cut his finger, __________ it isn't bleeding.
3. Mario likes spicy food, __________ he does not like peppers.
4. Ingrid __________ Delphine will sit with us.
5. Mom likes to watch dramas __________ mysteries.

C. Combine these sentences using **conjunctions**. **(7.8)**

1. Shane bought a hat. Shane bought a scarf.

____

2. James plays football. His sister plays basketball.

____

3. I like to sail. I get seasick.

____

Copyright 2006 Growing With Grammar Level 4. All Rights Reserved

D. Write the **fourth** column of **prepositions** from lesson **7.1**. **(7.1)**

____

____

____

____

____

____

____

____

____

____

____

E. Rewrite each sentence and add a **prepositional phrase** to give more detail. **(7.7)**

1. We met.

____

2. She found it.

____

F. **Diagram** these sentences. **(1.4, 4.2, 4.4, 5.2, 6.2, & 7.5)**

1. A cat ran out the door.

2. That girl moved to Alabama.

3. A cat with white paws ran.

4. That girl in the blue sweater is my friend.

Copyright 2006 Growing With Grammar Level 4. All Rights Reserved

Worksheet 7.9 (Interjections) Name______________________

A. Add an **interjection** to complete each sentence. **(7.9)**

1. ____________! I got chocolate on my new sweater!
2. ____________! You won the contest!
3. ____________! That food is spicy!
4. ____________! That hurt!
5. ____________! This food is disgusting!
6. ____________! That was hard work!

B. Write a sentence to go with each **interjection**. **(7.9)**

1. Look out! ______________________________
2. Stop! ______________________________
3. Finally! ______________________________
4. Terrific! ______________________________
5. Oh no! ______________________________
6. Yikes! ______________________________

C. Rewrite and change the punctuation in these sentences that have interjections. The words in parentheses will tell you whether to make each sentence a **strong interjection** or a **mild interjection**. **(7.9)**

1. Hurrah. We won the game. **(strong)**

____

2. Oh. It will be all right. **(mild)**

____

3. Whew. That was a close call. **(strong)**

____

Copyright 2006 Growing With Grammar Level 4. All Rights Reserved

D. Using **interjections**, write one sentence that expresses joy and one sentence that expresses pain. **(7.9)**

1. ____

____

2. ____

____

E. Write the **second**, **third**, and **fourth** columns of **prepositions** from lesson **7.1**. **(7.1)**

Column 1	Column 2	Column 3	Column 4
aboard	________	________	________
about	________	________	________
above	________	________	________
across	________	________	________
after	________	________	________
against	________	________	________
along	________	________	________
among	________	________	________
around		________	________
at		________	________
			________

F. Complete each of the following sentences with a **conjunction**. **(7.8)**

1. Marcos likes apples, __________ he can't stand applesauce.
2. Mr. Grayson is old __________ wise.
3. It was hot outside, __________ there was still snow on the ground.
4. Do you like swimming __________ skiing better?
5. Sharks are large, __________ they look fierce.
6. Was it your father __________ your mother who called?

Copyright 2006 Growing With Grammar Level 4. All Rights Reserved

Worksheet 7.10 (Of and Have) Name____________________________

A. Mark an **X** next to the sentences that are written correctly. **(7.10)**

1. _____ She could of bought a gift for Marnie.
2. _____ I would have gone skiing.
3. _____ We should have won the game.
4. _____ They could have been working.
5. _____ Jerry would of helped you.
6. _____ You should of passed that test.
7. _____ Mark could of arrived early.
8. _____ You should have stayed in bed longer.
9. _____ The boys could have gone fishing.
10. _____ I would have grabbed a sweater if I had known it was cold outside.
11. _____ I should of finished my homework.
12. _____ Brian would of gone with you.

B. Underline any **conjunction** in these sentences. **(7.8)**

1. We bought bowls and plates.
2. I like milk, but Jacob likes water.
3. Do you want a jacket or a sweater?
4. Tom planted trees, and Penny planted bushes.

C. Add an **interjection** to complete each sentence. **(7.9)**

1. ____________! I'm late again.
2. ____________! I won!
3. ____________! I forgot my money!
4. ____________! This is terrific!

Copyright 2006 Growing With Grammar Level 4. All Rights Reserved

D. Write the **fifth** column of **prepositions** from lesson **7.1**. **(7.1)**

____

____

____

____

____

____

____

____

____

____

E. Rewrite each sentence and add a **prepositional phrase** to give more detail. **(7.7)**

1. Mary walked.

____

2. The dog jumped.

____

F. **Diagram** these sentences. **(1.4, 1.12, 1.14, 4.2, 4.4, 5.2, 6.2, 6.6, & 7.5)**

1. Indra did not jump off the stage.

2. We bought our groceries at the store.

3. Jump in the pool.

4. Did you vote for her?

Copyright 2006 Growing With Grammar Level 4. All Rights Reserved

Worksheet 7.11 (Writing a Book Report) Name________________________

A. Answer the following questions about the **book report** example in lesson **7.11** of the student manual. **(7.11)**

1. Give the title and author of the book.

____

____

____

2. Where does the story take place?

____

____

3. Who are the main characters in the story?

____

____

____

4. Write one or two sentences from the report that describe the book.

____

____

____

____

____

5. What is the writer's opinion of the book? Does the writer recommend the book?

____

____

____

____

Copyright 2006 Growing With Grammar Level 4. All Rights Reserved

B. Mark an **X** next to the sentences that are written correctly. **(7.10)**

1. _____ You should of trimmed the hedges.

2. _____ Anthony could have made dinner.

3. _____ We would have taken you home.

4. _____ They could of gone skating.

5. _____ He should have told me he was sick.

C. Write the **third**, **fourth**, and **fifth** columns of **prepositions** from lesson **7.1**. **(7.1)**

Column 1	Column 2	Column 3	Column 4	Column 5
aboard	before	________	________	________
about	behind	________	________	________
above	below	________	________	________
across	beneath	________	________	________
after	beside	________	________	________
against	between	________	________	________
along	beyond	________	________	________
among	by	________	________	________
around		________	________	________
at		________	________	________
			________	

D. Write **P** if the word in bold is a **preposition**. Write **A** if it is an **adverb**. **Remember**: An **adverb** does **not** have an **object**. **(7.6)**

1. _________ The girls jogged **down** the street.

2. _________ Marie sat **down**.

3. _________ Let's go **inside**.

4. _________ Put the mail **inside** the mailbox.

Copyright 2006 Growing With Grammar Level 4. All Rights Reserved

Chapter 7 Review

Name____________________________

A. In each sentence, underline the **preposition** once and underline the **object of the preposition** twice. **(7.1)**

1. Jorge gave a report about iguanas.
2. The boy sat upon the stool.
3. We drove past a farm.
4. Bill arrived within nine minutes.
5. Outside the building we waited.
6. The cowboy jumped off his horse.

B. Draw a line under each **prepositional phrase**. Write the **preposition** on the line. **(7.2)**

1. Do you live by the river? ____________________
2. Jermaine went to the movie. ____________________
3. The boys were excited during the treasure hunt. ____________________
4. The stars appeared in the sky. ____________________
5. We watched the bird fly above our heads. ____________________
6. Dad bought a gift for me. ____________________

C. Underline the **adjective phrase**. Write the **noun** or **pronoun** it modifies on the line. (**Remember**, an adjective phrase **always** comes directly after the noun or pronoun it modifies.) **(7.3)**

1. The dictionary on the table is old. ____________________
2. An envelope with tickets arrived. ____________________
3. I own the bicycle with blue paint. ____________________
4. That butterfly with yellow wings is beautiful. ____________________
5. The soup of the day is chicken noodle. ____________________
6. The lady across the street is my aunt. ____________________

Copyright 2006 Growing With Grammar Level 4. All Rights Reserved

D. Underline each **adverb phrase** and write the **verb** it modifies on the line. (**Remember**, an adverb phrase can come at the **beginning** or the **end** of a sentence.) **(7.4)**

1. Yvonne slept after lunch. ______________________
2. We went to the store. ______________________
3. My cousin lives in Nebraska. ______________________
4. The hawk flew near us. ______________________
5. Margot talked to her father. ______________________
6. The squirrel climbed up the tree. ______________________

E. Write **P** if the word in bold is a **preposition**. Write **A** if it is an **adverb**. **Remember**: An **adverb** does **not** have an **object**. **(7.6)**

1. _________ The bookcase fell **over**.
2. _________ The girls looked **around**.
3. _________ He jogged **near** the road.
4. _________ We walked **over** the bridge.
5. _________ Does he live **near**?
6. _________ The bird flew **around** the room.

F. Rewrite each sentence and add a **prepositional phrase** to give more detail. **(7.7)**

Example: My friends traveled. → My friends **across the street** traveled.
-or- My friends traveled **to England**.

1. The boy rode a horse.

____

2. We bought food.

____

3. The cat sleeps.

____

Copyright 2006 Growing With Grammar Level 4. All Rights Reserved

G. Combine these sentences using **conjunctions**. (7.8)

1. Kittens run. Kittens play.

____

2. The book was very old. The writing had not faded.

____

3. Mary went to the ball game. Jimmy went to the ball game.

____

H. Add an **interjection** to complete each sentence. (7.9)

1. ____________! I need help fast!
2. ____________! That bee stung me!
3. ____________! This is easy!
4. ____________! The baby is sleeping.
5. ____________! This road is dangerous!

I. **Diagram** these sentences. (1.4, 1.12, 1.14, 4.2, 4.4, 5.2, 6.2, 6.6, & 7.5)

1. We went to the store.

2. An envelope with tickets arrived.

3. The hawk flew near us.

4. The lady across the street is my aunt.

Copyright 2006 Growing With Grammar Level 4. All Rights Reserved

Copyright 2006 Growing With Grammar Level 4. All Rights Reserved

Worksheet 8.1 (Prefixes) Name______________________

A. Write the correct word for each meaning below by using the word in bold as a base word and adding the **prefix im-**, **dis-**, or **pre-**. **(8.1)**

1. not **possible** ______________________
2. not **honest** ______________________
3. **pay** before ______________________
4. not **patient** ______________________
5. to not **like** ______________________
6. **heat** before ______________________
7. not **mature** ______________________
8. not **obey** ______________________
9. **plan** before ______________________
10. not **polite** ______________________

B. Circle the correct meaning for each word. **(8.1)**

1. discontinued	→	continued before	not continued
2. preview	→	not view	view before
3. immobile	→	mobile before	not mobile
4. disrespectful	→	not respectful	respectful before
5. prepackage	→	package before	not package
6. improper	→	not proper	proper before
7. disagree	→	agree before	not agree
8. prearrange	→	arrange before	not arrange
9. impersonal	→	not personal	personal before
10. disconnected	→	not connected	connected before

Copyright 2006 Growing With Grammar Level 4. All Rights Reserved

C. Write the meaning for each word. **(8.1)**

1. disloyal ______________________________
2. impossible ______________________________
3. preapprove ______________________________
4. distrust ______________________________
5. imperfect ______________________________
6. precook ______________________________
7. disbelieve ______________________________
8. immature ______________________________
9. preplan ______________________________
10. dissatisfied ______________________________

D. Add the **prefix im-**, **dis-**, or **pre-** to each of words below. Then write a sentence using the new word. **(8.1)**

1. _________honest

____

____

____

2. _________heat

____

____

____

Copyright 2006 Growing With Grammar Level 4. All Rights Reserved

Worksheet 8.2 (Rise and Raise) Name________________________

A. Mark an **X** next to the sentences that are written correctly. **(8.2)**

1. _____ We rise to our feet to applaud.
2. _____ Marianne is rising her hand.
3. _____ Will you raise the flag?
4. _____ Store owners are raising prices.
5. _____ Smoke raises into the air.
6. _____ The bread is rising on the counter.
7. _____ The river raises every spring.
8. _____ Eleanor likes to rise early.

B. Write **rise** or **raise** to complete each sentence. Underline the **direct objects** in the sentences that require the verb **raise**. **(8.2)**

1. The girls will ____________________ the curtain before the play.
2. The sun will ____________________ soon.
3. ____________________ your hand as a signal.
4. Our landlord said she will ____________________ the rent.
5. We watched the smoke ____________________ from the fire.
6. The children ____________________ from the bench.
7. Will you help me ____________________ money for my trip?
8. The boys ____________________ chickens on the farm.
9. The river will ____________________ during the storm.
10. The moon will ____________________ early tonight.

Copyright 2006 Growing With Grammar Level 4. All Rights Reserved

C. Circle the correct word for each sentence. **(8.2)**

1. When does the moon (raise, rise)?
2. Edward always (raises, rises) his eyebrows when he's surprised.
3. The fog is (raising, rising).
4. Please do not (raise, rise) your voice.
5. The man (raises, rises) from his chair.
6. The girl is (raising, rising) her hand.

D. **Diagram** these sentences. **(1.4, 1.12, 1.14, 4.2, 4.4, 5.2, 6.2, 6.6, & 7.5)**

1. The small dog raced around the yard.
2. My cousin from Italy stayed with our family.
3. I wrote a story about my family.
4. The animal in the cage is a ferret.

Copyright 2006 Growing With Grammar Level 4. All Rights Reserved

Worksheet 8.3 (Let and Leave) Name__________________________

A. Mark an **X** next to the sentences that are written correctly. **(8.3)**

1. ______ Leave the door open.
2. ______ Let me alone!
3. ______ I hope you leave him go to the movies.
4. ______ I leave tomorrow.
5. ______ Let me go!
6. ______ She always leaves her umbrella at home.
7. ______ Leave her go by herself.
8. ______ Let the cat in.

B. Write **let** or **leave** to complete each sentence. **(8.3)**

1. Will you _______________________ him take your picture?
2. Please _______________________ her alone while she is reading.
3. _______________________ me stay here by myself.
4. We will _______________________ the house in two hours.
5. _______________________ me tell you a story.
6. You can _______________________ your shoes here.
7. Will you _______________________ us go to the park?
8. Did you _______________________ the window open all night?
9. _______________________ me alone!
10. _______________________ me go with you!

Copyright 2006 Growing With Grammar Level 4. All Rights Reserved

C. Circle the correct word for each sentence. **(8.2 & 8.3)**

1. (Let, Leave) me have another piece of pie.
2. Please don't (raise, rise) your voice.
3. Vanessa is (letting, leaving) in the morning.
4. The smoke is (raising, rising) from the volcano.
5. Mom always (lets, leaves) us go to the pool.
6. Grandpa (raises, rises) pigs on his farm.
7. Did you (let, leave) your shoes out in the rain?
8. He will (raise, rise) before dawn to go to work.
9. Thank you for (letting, leaving) me borrow your book.
10. We will be (raising, rising) the flag on Flag Day.

D. Rewrite these sentences using proper **capitalization** and **punctuation.**
(1.11, 1.15, 2.9, & 3.7 - 3.10)

1. mia did you take jessica's doll asked mrs johnson

   ____

2. canadian citizens sometimes fly south for the winter

   ____

3. is the coliseum in rome

   ____

4. jason went rafting on the colorado river in may

   ____

Copyright 2006 Growing With Grammar Level 4. All Rights Reserved

Worksheet 8.4 (Lend and Borrow) Name______________________________

A. Mark an **X** next to the sentences that are written correctly. **(8.4)**

1. ______ Lend me your sweater.
2. ______ Jeff borrows his pencil to me.
3. ______ Do you need to lend some money from me?
4. ______ We borrow books from the library.
5. ______ Should I borrow my ruler to her?
6. ______ I am lending my bike to Mary.
7. ______ Mom needs to borrow some sugar from our neighbor.
8. ______ He lends tools from his father.

B. Write **lend** or **borrow** to complete each sentence. **(8.4)**

1. Maurice will ______________________ a bike to his brother.
2. She likes to ______________________ books from the library.
3. Sandy will ______________________ a microscope from the school.
4. He needs to ______________________ some money for his new game.
5. I will ______________________ a hammer to my uncle.
6. She will ______________________ her skates to him.
7. Can I ______________________ that recipe from you?
8. Sylvia will ______________________ her hat to you.
9. Will you ______________________ me a pen?
10. Bryan is going to ______________________ five dollars from me.

Copyright 2006 Growing With Grammar Level 4. All Rights Reserved

C. Circle the correct word for each sentence. **(8.2 , 8.3, & 8.4)**

1. Can I (lend, borrow) your sweater from you?
2. (Let, Leave) the squirrels alone.
3. Mom likes to (raise, rise) her own tomatoes.
4. Joy is (lending, borrowing) books from the library.
5. Grandpa is (letting, leaving) today.
6. Smoke is (raising, rising) from the campfire.
7. The bank (lends, borrows) money to people.
8. Dad (lets, leaves) us stay up late on Saturdays.
9. Martha (raises, rises) her voice when she is angry.
10. Did you (lend, borrow) a notebook from Gwyn?

D. Add words after each preposition to complete these sentences. Underline the **preposition** once and the **object of the preposition** twice. **(7.1)**

Example: The story was about → The story was about **a parade**.

1. The children climbed inside ____________________________________.
2. I just saw Joe running toward ____________________________________.
3. The pencil is lying on ____.
4. We rode our bikes around ______________________________________.
5. Your shoes are behind ____.
6. The baby threw her bottle against ________________________________.
7. We had a picnic in ____.
8. Did you look underneath ______________________________________?

Copyright 2006 Growing With Grammar Level 4. All Rights Reserved

Worksheet 8.5 (Using Teach and Learn) Name________________________

A. Mark an **X** next to the sentences that are written correctly. **(8.5)**

1. _____ My mother is teaching me how to speak Spanish.
2. _____ She is learning the dolphins how to jump through the hoop.
3. _____ Elisa learns her sister how to tie her shoes.
4. _____ I learn a new word everyday.
5. _____ Will you teach me how to ride a skateboard?
6. _____ Uncle Phil is learning us how to change a flat tire.
7. _____ He taught Bob how to surf.
8. _____ I am learning myself how to type.

B. Write **teach** or **learn** to complete each sentence. **(8.5)**

1. Roy will ____________________ his brother to ride a bike.
2. Nima likes to ____________________ other people.
3. I want to ____________________ how to windsurf.
4. Will you ____________________ me how to make bread?
5. Margo will ____________________ the boys to cook.
6. Francisco will ____________________ a new way to tie a knot.
7. Can you ____________________ an old dog new tricks?
8. Dad will ____________________ us how to fish.
9. My parents ____________________ us how to save money.
10. What will we ____________________ about today?

Copyright 2006 Growing With Grammar Level 4. All Rights Reserved

C. Circle the correct word for each sentence. **(8.2 , 8.3, 8.4, & 8.5)**

1. Can you (teach, learn) the dog to fetch?
2. I need to (lend, borrow) your radio.
3. (Let, Leave) him alone!
4. (Raise, Rise) your hand if you have a question.
5. Tonya is (teaching, learning) from her sister how to do a cartwheel.
6. Sarah always (lends, borrows) money to her sister.
7. The river (raises, rises) after every storm.
8. (Let, Leave) him go with you.

D. **Diagram** these sentences. **(1.4, 1.12, 1.14, 4.2, 4.4, 5.2, 6.2, 6.6, & 7.5)**

1. Dory walked behind the blue house.
3. Rake those leaves into a pile.

2. Around the track Jani and Kyla raced.
4. Did you find those shells on the beach?

Copyright 2006 Growing With Grammar Level 4. All Rights Reserved

Worksheet 8.6 (Troublesome Words) Name________________________

A. Write **to**, **too**, or **two** on the line to complete each sentence. **(8.6)**

1. Sam walked ____________________ the store.
2. My bedroom has ____________________ windows.
3. Did Alan leave, ____________________?
4. This recipe requires____________________ cups of flour.
5. There are ____________________ eggs in the nest.
6. Mindy was ____________________ frightened to ask for help.
7. Tomorrow we are going ____________________ New York.
8. Are you going ____________________ the game?
9. I have ____________________ much food on my plate.
10. Emma's sister is ____________________ years old.

B. Circle the correct word for each sentence. **(8.6)**

1. The players threw (there, their, they're) mitts into the air.
2. (There, Their, They're) are three raccoons in the yard.
3. I think (there, their, they're) waiting for us.
4. The lightning struck (there, their, they're).
5. (There, Their, They're) shoes were covered with mud.
6. Put the garbage can over (there, their, they're).
7. (There, Their, They're) having a cookout tonight.
8. (There, Their, They're) learning about the weather.
9. (There, Their, They're) mother is an attorney.
10. (There, Their, They're) aren't any cookies left.

Copyright 2006 Growing With Grammar Level 4. All Rights Reserved

C. Circle the correct word for each sentence. **(8.2 , 8.3, 8.4, 8.5, & 8.6)**

1. We are going to (rise, raise) chickens this year.
2. (Let, Leave) me stay here by myself.
3. (There, Their, They're) taking their uncle to the airport.
4. Do you have (to, too, two) nickels?
5. May I (lend, borrow) your eraser.
6. He is (teaching, learning) them how to mow the lawn.
7. Would you like to come (to, too, two)?
8. (There, Their, They're) aunt is an opera singer.

D. Write three sentences about how to make a new friend. Be sure to use the words **there**, **their**, and **they're** in your sentences. **(8.6)**

____

____

____

____

____

____

____

____

____

____

Copyright 2006 Growing With Grammar Level 4. All Rights Reserved

Worksheet 8.7 (More Troublesome Words) Name____________________________

A. Write **it's** or **its** to complete each sentence. **(8.7)**

1. ____________________ time to leave.
2. The dog likes to chase ____________________ tail.
3. ____________________ raining outside.
4. I think ____________________ my turn to bat.
5. ____________________ too bad you can't go to the museum.
6. The bear turned ____________________ back to us.
7. ____________________ a good day to play at the park.
8. The car flipped over on ____________________ side.
9. ____________________ Matteo's turn.
10. The cat lost ____________________ collar.

B. Write **you're** or **your** to complete each sentence. **(8.7)**

1. ____________________ sister said you saw a coyote.
2. ____________________ answer is correct.
3. ____________________ a very smart girl.
4. Please put ____________________ name on the paper.
5. ____________________ going to love the movie.
6. ____________________ shirt is ripped.
7. I think that ____________________ hilarious!
8. ____________________ the tallest of the three girls.
9. ____________________ house is bigger than ours.
10. ____________________ the winner of the race!

Copyright 2006 Growing With Grammar Level 4. All Rights Reserved

C. Write **who's** or **whose** to compete each sentence. **(8.7)**

1. ____________________ kitten is that?
2. ____________________ the person in charge?
3. ____________________ taking us home?
4. ____________________ the winner?
5. ____________________ he taking to the movies?
6. ____________________ basketball is this?
7. ____________________ next in line?
8. ____________________ hat is this?

D. Rewrite each sentence and add a **prepositional phrase** to give more detail. **(7.7)**

Example: The girl drove there. → The girl **in the red car** drove there.
-or- The girl drove there **in a rainstorm**.

1. My kite crashed.

____

2. You may go.

____

3. We have to wait.

____

4. The mouse ran.

____

Copyright 2006 Growing With Grammar Level 4. All Rights Reserved

Worksheet 8.8 (Abbreviations) Name____________________________

A. Write the **abbreviations** for these words or names. **(8.8)**

1. New Mexico ____________________
2. Doctor ____________________
3. Road ____________________
4. Building ____________________
5. Senior ____________________
6. Drive ____________________
7. Pennsylvania ____________________
8. Mistress ____________________
9. Alberta ____________________
10. Attorney ____________________
11. Mister ____________________
12. Avenue ____________________
13. Province ____________________
14. President ____________________
15. Apartment ____________________
16. Junior ____________________
17. Captain ____________________
18. Puerto Rico ____________________
19. Highway ____________________
20. Route ____________________

B. Write the word for each **abbreviation**. **(8.8)**

1. DC ____
2. Natl. ____
3. Sen. ____
4. St. ____
5. Mt. ____
6. IN ____
7. CA ____
8. Sgt. ____
9. Dist. ____
10. Terr. ____

Copyright 2006 Growing With Grammar Level 4. All Rights Reserved

C. Rewrite these **names** and **titles** using correct punctuation and **abbreviations**. **(8.8)**

1. t j parker ______________________
2. doctor g basil ______________________
3. mister johnson ______________________
4. robert a hogan, senior ______________________
5. mistress julia gilbert ______________________
6. senator kline ______________________
7. 123 Main street ______________________
8. reverend b michaels ______________________

D. **Diagram** these sentences. **(1.4, 1.12, 1.14, 4.2, 4.4, 5.2, 6.2, 6.6, & 7.5)**

1. Two ducks flew away.

2. The girl in the red car drove there.

3. My sister is leaving tomorrow.

4. The man ran there in a rainstorm.

Copyright 2006 Growing With Grammar Level 4. All Rights Reserved

Worksheet 8.9 (More Abbreviations) Name________________________

A. Write the **unit of measure** that each **abbreviation** stands for. **(8.9)**

1. doz. ________________
2. in. ________________
3. mi. ________________
4. yd. ________________
5. tsp. ________________
6. gal. ________________
7. ft. ________________
8. qt. ________________
9. lb. ________________
10. pt. ________________
11. oz. ________________
12. tbsp. ________________

B. Write the **abbreviations** for these **calendar items**. **(8.9)**

1. February ________________
2. Sunday ________________
3. September ________________
4. year ________________
5. November ________________
6. Saturday ________________
7. October ________________
8. Tuesday ________________
9. Thursday ________________
10. month ________________
11. Friday ________________
12. Monday ________________
13. December ________________
14. Wednesday ________________
15. January ________________
16. April ________________
17. August ________________
18. March ________________

C. Write the **abbreviations** for **time**. **(8.9)**

1. before noon ________________ or ________________
2. after noon ________________ or ________________
3. second ________________
4. hour ________________
5. minute ________________

Copyright 2006 Growing With Grammar Level 4. All Rights Reserved

D. Answer these questions using the correct **abbreviations**. **(8.8 & 8.9)**

1. How do you write your name using initials? ______________________
2. What is the current time? ______________________
3. What is your birth month? ______________________
4. What day of the week is it today? ______________________
5. What is your home state or province? ______________________
6. How tall are you in inches? ______________________
7. How much do you weigh in pounds? ______________________
8. How old are you in years? ______________________
9. What is your street address?

____

10. What is your doctor's or teacher's name using a title?

____

E. Circle the correct word for each sentence. **(8.6 & 8.7)**

1. This movie is (to, too, two) long.
2. I want to go (there, their, they're).
3. (It's, Its) not too late to change your mind.
4. I have (to, too, two) extra tickets for the ballet.
5. (Who's, Whose) cat is that?
6. Have you gone (to, too, two) Missy's house?
7. I think (there, their, they're) going to California.
8. (You're, Your) my best friend.
9. Is that (there, their, they're) father?
10. The dog dropped (it's, its) bone.

Copyright 2006 Growing With Grammar Level 4. All Rights Reserved

Worksheet 8.10 (Commas) Name_______________________

A. Place **commas** where needed in each sentence. **(8.10)**

1. The horse neighed kicked and snorted.
2. Brian Roger Robin and Mason were at the ceremony.
3. Belle washed the dishes and I vacuumed the stairs.
4. On Tuesday January 20 my sister was born.
5. Uncle Thomas moved to Detroit Michigan.
6. Alex looked for his lost toy but he could not find it.
8. Rebecca have the plants been watered today?
9. Cows pigs donkeys and chickens live on that farm.
10. Well I think it is time for you to leave.
11. I'm very happy for you Irene.
12. Is Seoul South Korea the largest city in Asia?
13. No you did not win the contest.
14. It has not rained for two weeks but the river is still very high.
15. Mrs. James is a wife mother sister and aunt.
16. Do you think Mom that I can make dinner?
17. April 23 1949 is when my grandparents were married.
18. The pitcher catcher and outfielder called a time out.
19. Yes he does like broccoli.
20. Roses bloom in the summer but leaves change color in the fall.

Copyright 2006 Growing With Grammar Level 4. All Rights Reserved

B. Add **commas** where needed in these letter parts. **(8.10)**

1. Dear Elizabeth
2. March 17 20--
3. Raleigh NC
4. Your friend
5. Dear Aunt Emma
6. Sincerely
7. November 2 20--
8. Paris France
9. Miami FL
10. Dear Robert
11. September 19 20--
12. Your pen pal
13. Dearest Darcy
14. Dallas TX
15. Calcutta India
16. Best regards
17. Cairo Egypt
18. May 11 20--
19. Dear Grandma Ruth
20. Your cousin

C. Write a sentence listing your four favorite foods. Write another sentence listing your three closest friends. Add **commas** where needed. **(8.10)**

____

____

____

____

____

____

Copyright 2006 Growing With Grammar Level 4. All Rights Reserved

Chapter 8 Review

Name______________________________

A. Write the correct word for each meaning below by using the word in bold as a base word and adding the **prefix im-**, **dis-**, or **pre-**. **(8.1)**

1. not **perfect** ______________________________
2. **pay** before ______________________________
3. not **satisfied** ______________________________
4. not **personal** ______________________________
5. **cook** before ______________________________
6. not **honest** ______________________________

B. Circle the correct word for each sentence. **(8.2 , 8.3, 8.4, 8.5, 8.6, & 8.7)**

1. The sun will (rise, raise) in the east.
2. (Let, Leave) me do it again!
3. I have (to, too, two) brothers.
4. (There, Their, They're) playing checkers.
5. Can I (lend, borrow) your pencil?
6. Dad will (teach, learn) us how to ski.
7. We are going (to, too, two) the museum.
8. He put the keys (there, their, they're).
9. (It's, Its) too hot outside.
10. (You're, Your) a great singer!
11. (Who's, Whose) bicycle is this?
12. They were (to, too, two) late.
13. The children forgot (there, their, they're) mittens.
14. The penguin lowered (it's, its) head.
15. Is that (you're, your) mother?
16. (Who's, Whose) coming to pick us up?

Copyright 2006 Growing With Grammar Level 4. All Rights Reserved

C. Write the **abbreviations** for these words or names properly. **(8.8)**

1. Texas ____________________
2. Professor ____________________
3. Avenue ____________________
4. Hawaii ____________________
5. Captain ____________________
6. Drive ____________________
7. Mistress ____________________
8. Junior ____________________
9. Building ____________________
10. Route ____________________
11. Senior ____________________
12. Highway ____________________

D. Rewrite these **names** and **titles** using correct punctuation and **abbreviations**. **(8.8)**

1. mister c w childs ____________________
2. doctor avery ____________________
3. omar j robins, junior ____________________
4. mistress c Webster ____________________
5. 23 Pine avenue ____________________
6. p john elliot, senior ____________________

E. Write the **unit of measure** that each **abbreviation** stands for. **(8.9)**

1. oz. ____________________
2. ft. ____________________
3. doz. ____________________
4. tsp. ____________________
5. yd. ____________________
6. qt. ____________________
7. mi. ____________________
8. lb. ____________________
9. gal. ____________________
10. pt. ____________________
11. tbsp. ____________________
12. in. ____________________

Copyright 2006 Growing With Grammar Level 4. All Rights Reserved

F. Write the **abbreviations** for these **calendar items**. **(8.9)**

1. September ________________
2. Thursday ________________
3. month ________________
4. March ________________
5. Sunday ________________
6. February ________________
7. year ________________
8. November ________________
9. Saturday ________________
10. Tuesday ________________
11. October ________________
12. Friday ________________

G. Write the **abbreviations** for **time**. **(8.9)**

1. before noon ________________ or ________________
2. after noon ________________ or ________________
3. second ________________
4. hour ________________
5. minute ________________

H. Place **commas** where needed in each sentence. **(8.10)**

1. Helen are you feeling well?
2. Michael drinks only water but Philip will drink almost anything.
3. Next week we will be visiting Houston Texas.
4. The children ran laughed and played.
5. Yes we are performing in the play.
6. Hornets bees and wasps will sting.
7. The players entered the arena and the crowd cheered.
8. I like your earrings Kimberly.

Copyright 2006 Growing With Grammar Level 4. All Rights Reserved

<This page intentionally left blank>

Copyright 2006 Growing With Grammar Level 4. All Rights Reserved